Dannah and Juli pull back the shades to shine some light on how erotic literature exploits the deep spiritual and sexual longings of a woman's heart. With the Bible as a mooring, they help us address these longings in healthy and holy ways. If you've read erotica, have been tempted to read it, or are even mildly curious about it, you MUST read this book!

—**MARY KASSIAN**, author, *Girls Gone Wise*

Dannah and Juli have created a beautiful guide book for real intimacy that satisfies our deepest longings. They debunk the lies we naively trade for the Truth. Open the pages of this book to discover the satisfaction you deeply long for.

—**JILL SAVAGE**, founder and CEO of
Hearts at Home, author of nine books
including *No More Perfect Moms*

Sexual pleasure is not about self-gratification, and it is more than mutual gratification. Single or married, we are called to be spiritually, relationally, and sexually mature, for the glory of God! Whether man or woman, our sinful natures can easily lead us into the false intimacy of BDSM. *Pulling Back the Shades* exposes the myths of *Fifty Shades of Grey*. This book will lead many who have fallen into the darkness back into a passion for God's glory with both a strong mature spiritual and sexual desire.

—**HARRY W. SCHAUMBURG**, founder of Stone
Gate Resources, author of *False Intimacy* and
Undefiled

Do you long to be a spiritually satisfied woman? Do you long to be a sexually satisfied woman? *Pulling Back the Shades* will take you to new places in spiritual and sexual freedom (and it's not to a Red Room of Pain!).

> —LINDA DILLOW, speaker and bestselling author of *Calm My Anxious Heart* and *What's It Like to Be Married to Me?*

You may be surprised that this is a gracious, sensitive, encouraging, and direct (but not embarrassing) book. Dannah and Juli have tackled a tough topic but do so in a compassionate manner, examining the consequences of a trend that may seem new but was just as much of a challenge to first-century Christians as it is today. The temptation is timeless, but so is the solution. Single women, teens, wives, mothers, aunts, grandmothers, sisters . . . this one's for you.

> —CAROLYN MCCULLEY, author of *The Measure of Success, Radical Womanhood, Did I Kiss Marriage Goodbye?*

Our culture is changing and the blurry lines of what is "right" and "wrong" are confusing to many. It is time for Christian women to take a stand for what is true, right, and holy. Dannah and Juli challenge us all to lead lives that are above reproach without a hint of sexual immorality. This book is a call to influence, with biblical guidelines, our culture by living lives as wise, godly, and pure women.

> —BETH LUEBE, The Collegiate Navigators

Pulling Back
the Shades

EROTICA, INTIMACY, AND THE
LONGINGS OF A WOMAN'S HEART

Dannah Gresh
and
Dr. Juli Slattery

MOODY PUBLISHERS
CHICAGO

All Scripture quotation, unless otherwise indicated, are taken from the *Holy Bible, New International Version*®, NIV®. Copyright © 1973, 1978, 1984, 2011 by Biblica, Inc.™ Used by permission of Zondervan. All rights reserved worldwide. www.zondervan.com. The "NIV" and "New International Version" are trademarks registered in the United States Patent and Trademark Office by Biblica, Inc.™

Scripture quotations marked NLT are taken from the Holy Bible, New Living Translation, copyright © 1996, 2004, 2007 by Tyndale House Foundation. Used by permission of Tyndale House Publishers, Inc., Wheaton, Illinois 60188. All rights reserved.

Scripture quotations marked THE MESSAGE are from *The Message*, copyright © by Eugene H. Peterson 1993, 1994, 1995. Used by permission of NavPress Publishing Group.

Edited by Terry Behimer
Interior design: Ragont Design
Cover design: DBA Faceout Studio
Cover images: Mask: Shutterstock #41846107;
            Ribbon: Shutterstock #120381373
Author Photos: Dannah Gresh-Steve Smith / Juli Slattery-Cathy Walters

Library of Congress Cataloging-in-Publication Data

Slattery, Julianna
    Pulling back the shades : erotica, intimacy, and the longings of a woman's heart / Dr. Juli Slattery and Dannah Gresh.
        pages cm
    Includes bibliographical references.
    ISBN 978-0-8024-1088-7
    1. Sex—Religious aspects—Christianity. 2. Christian women—Sexual behavior. 3. Christian women—Religious life. I. Title.
    BT708.S545 2014
    241'.664082—dc23

                                                              2013047171

All websites and phone numbers listed herein are accurate at the time of publication but may change in the future or cease to exist. The listing of website references and resources does not imply publisher endorsement of the site's entire contents. Groups and organizations are listed for informational purposes, and listing does not imply publisher endorsement of their activities

We hope you enjoy this book from Moody Publishers. Our goal is to provide high-quality, thought-provoking books and products that connect truth to your real needs and challenges. For more information on other books and products written and produced from a biblical perspective, go to www.moodypublishers.com or write to:

Moody Publishers
820 N. LaSalle Boulevard
Chicago, IL 60610

5 7 9 10 8 6 4

Printed in the United States of America

CONTENTS

True Confessions from Dannah & Juli   9

1. We Know Why You Read It   15

2. Fifty Shades of Deception   29

3. Why Mommy Porn Is Spiritual   41

4. Some Things Really Are Black and White   57

5. Since When Does Prince Charming
   Carry Handcuffs?   75

6. Don't Let the Red Room Destroy Your Bedroom   89

7. The Sexually Satisfied Woman   101

8. The Spiritually Satisfied Woman   117

9. Reviving More than Your Sex Life   133

Questions for Group Discussion   151

Appendix 1: Practical Resources   157

Appendix 2: What Do I Do with My Struggle?
Practical Ideas for Victory   161

Notes   167

Acknowledgments   171

True Confessions
from Dannah & Juli

This is a book we never expected to write about a book we never expected you to read: *Fifty Shades of Grey*. How could a *poorly written* book series have sold over 70 million copies in its first year? And now it's not just that series being devoured by women, but an entire lineup of copycat books rushed to the market so fast that the BBC reported erotica to be "cannibalizing" the rest of the publishing industry. Erotica is the fastest-selling genre of books selling to women.

We believe that the release of the Fifty Shades of Grey series was a transforming moment that fueled the erotica craze, normalizing its use. The series has done for women and erotica what the advent of the Internet did for men and porn.

Some consider the story of Christian and Anastasia, the hero and protagonist in the Fifty Shades series, to be one of love and healing. Others say it's degrading and pornographic. There are plenty of opinions on both sides of the debate and no doubt you have yours. (And, you should know, ours is based only on the books because we haven't viewed the movie.) But before we dive into our opinions, we have to stop and confess a few things about our initial reactions to the movement.

◆ ◆ ◆

I, Dannah, was introduced to the book by my husband, who'd been hearing about it in the media buzz. One night he couldn't take it anymore.

"You've got to write about this book," Bob said incredulously. He plopped a laptop in front of me and pushed play. A *Saturday Night Live* commercial spoof for amazon.com began. It was advertising a book I'd never heard of before: *Fifty Shades of Grey*.

A woman was reading the book in a bathtub and masturbating, when her husband and son walked in on her. She hollered and acted ashamed. Another woman was reading the book while she used her clothes washer as a vibrator, when her husband walked in on her. She hollered and acted ashamed. Another woman was reading the book and using a vibrator in bed, when her husband and kids came in with breakfast in bed for Mother's Day. She hollered and acted ashamed.

I pushed the computer away and told my husband matter-of-factly, "Oh, honey, I'm not going to write about that. I don't think that many spiritual women will be attracted to it."

The next day my mom told me a friend of hers had read it.

The next week a friend of mine told me her seventy-year-old mother had her name on a very long list at the library to get it.

The conversation had begun and it seemed everywhere I turned, a friend, family member, or acquaintance was either reading the books or asking if they should. Some of them specifically mentioned that they were excited that people were *finally* talking about topics like spanking.

10

Spiritual women, all of them.

Apparently, as a sexuality expert and relationship coach to spiritual women, I did need to write about this. So I wrote a blog titled "I'm Not Reading *Fifty Shades of Grey*." It sparked a fuel-fire of controversy with over fourteen hundred women choosing to pound out their opinions, long paragraph followed by long paragraph. Some defended the book and their choice to read it and criticized me for being judgmental. Others applauded me. Many wondered how I could critique it without having ever read it.

But I still haven't.

What I have read are the stories of countless women who *have* read *Fifty Shades of Grey* or other books in the erotica genre. It turns out I was very wrong: spiritual women *do* read erotica.

Praying grandmas are reading it.

Vibrant young human-trafficking activists are reading it.

Pastors' wives are reading it.

Homeschooled teenage girls are reading it.

The heads of charitable foundations are reading it.

Missionaries are reading it.

Professors of religion are reading it.

Jews, Muslims, and Christians are reading it.

I thought long and hard before I decided not to read it. While one obvious reason was that I'd already publicly stated that I wouldn't, another was that I want to dispel the myth that you have to read it to be able to have an informed opinion and engage in the debate. I have taken the time to come at this debate from another angle by engaging in the stories of women whose lives have been impacted by erotica. Email by email, they poured their hearts out. Many of them were brave enough to tell their stories, some of which you'll read in this book.

My friend Juli took a different approach.

❖ ❖ ❖

I, Juli, am a clinical psychologist and the cofounder of a ministry that focuses on intimacy for women. The Fifty Shades phenomenon had my attention right away. Frankly, I thought it was a passing fad. I never dreamed it would catch fire as it has.

I began to write and do interviews about the book series and stated that I would not be reading them. Some women responded with comments like, "How can you know they are bad if you don't read them? It's really a love story!"

When I sensed the Lord prompting me and Dannah to write this book, I realized I would have to read Fifty Shades. I was very reluctant. My husband, Mike, and I have worked hard over the years to develop a fulfilling and pure sex life. I didn't want to take the risk of reading something that might taint what we had fought to secure. So with lots of prayer cover, I began to read the books, asking God to give me His wisdom to discern truth.

These books are not black and white. Woven throughout their countless and graphic sexual encounters, Christian and

Ana are seeking love. One might even argue that they end up healing each other in this strange, fictional world. Even though I read the books in a spirit of prayer—literally on my knees—I got pulled into the story. My body even got pulled in. There were times while reading the series that I was appalled by the graphic and twisted sexual scenes—but I was also aroused. These books are powerful and had a significant impact on me. I find it difficult to believe women who say, "I read all three books. They didn't really affect me." I want to say, "Then why did you read all three? Something kept your attention!"

❖   ❖   ❖

In the pages ahead, we'll embark on the journey of *Pulling Back the Shades*. You might consider this a double play on words. Not only do we want to pull back the shades of *Grey* for you to see God's truth about what it and other books like it can do in your life, but we also want to pull back the shades on your own sex life. This book is not meant to be merely a reaction to the Fifty Shades of Grey series. Ultimately it is about YOU—your longings, your questions, and your wholeness as a spiritual and sexual woman. We hope to offer you something you deeply need.

We believe God has called us to write this book together. We both feel very burdened about the impact of Fifty Shades and want to help you sort out truth from fiction in real life. As we began to work on writing, we noticed that God has given us different passions and "voices" about this topic.

Instead of trying to blend our thoughts, we are approaching this like a conversation. So, Dannah's writing will be in this font. Juli's writing will be in this font.

Together, we have sought God for His wisdom for you, a woman He loves deeply. While Fifty Shades has changed the sexual landscape for many women, we pray that *this* book is also a game changer—bringing hope and healing through the power of God's truth.

Chapter 1

We Know Why You Read It

We want to let you in on a little secret: it's possible to be a spiritual woman and to struggle with sexual issues.

Homeschoolers (both moms *and* students), Bible study teachers, missionaries, college students, single business-women, married stay-at-home moms, and praying grandmothers who are actively serving the Lord have sexual struggles.

Desperate longings to be touched by a man.

Online temptation.

Disappointment in a marriage bed.

Physical loneliness.

Left with no one to talk to, a woman can end up turning sexual struggles into shameful secrets.

Having sex outside of marriage.

Conducting a secret online affair.

Becoming addicted to porn.

For so long it's been unacceptable in the Christian community for a spiritual woman to openly admit to these sexual secrets. Then along came *Fifty Shades of Grey*—a book offering a bounty of explicit, erotic sex scenes all wrapped up in a love story. Suddenly, there is a sexual outlet for the spiritual woman that seems to be perfectly acceptable. Their longings and fantasies finally have a place to be expressed in erotica, which promises to revive sexual passion in marriage or chan-nel sexual desire for singles.

We want you to know you're not alone. Spiritual women *do* struggle with sexual shame. We've heard from so many of you, and your hearts are eager for some answers—answers that the church traditionally was not willing to provide because it was afraid to talk about the very things you need desperately for us to talk about.

So, along with a growing number of increasingly transpar-ent Christian leaders, we intend to approach this topic quite differently. Why? Because Jesus did.

Jesus met a woman at a well who was never going to be satisfied drinking at the well of sexual expression to satisfy her emotional thirst (we'll share more about her in chapter 8). When He approached her, He broke racial, religious, and sexual traditions. Those customs were not as important to Him as rescuing the woman with Living Water.

We may break a few unwritten, man-made, but nonethe-less "Christian rules" of the past in the pages of this book. No conversation will be taboo if it can rescue your heart and bring you to the Living Water.

We have already gone to great lengths to bring you hope, including the decision that Juli would actually read the Fifty Shades of Grey series. With her heart in an attitude of prayer and her psychologist's hat on, she went where neither of us really wanted to go. While doing so, she identified five unmet longings in women, based on the roller-coaster ride of emo-tions she personally experienced as she read the series, coupled with her years as a counselor.

At the same time, I identified five characteristics of successful erotica, based on interviews of those who read it and the writing guidelines given to authors in the industry (known as "sexperts").

We came at these lists completely independent of each other. Take a look at how our lists matched up.

A WOMAN'S FIVE LONGINGS	CHARACTERISTICS OF SUCCESSFUL EROTICA
To escape reality.	Focuses on female fantasy.
To be cherished by a man.	Presents an *innocent* female protagonist who makes a man forget other women even exist.
To be protected by a strong man.	Presents a controlling alpha male who dominates the female.
To rescue a man.	Characterizes the female protagonist as the only one who can meet the deepest, darkest needs of a man.
To be sexually alive.	Offers detailed descriptions of sex.

❖   ❖   ❖

We know that women aren't just drawn into books like *Fifty Shades of Grey* for the entertainment value. Erotica strategically and masterfully pulls you in by exploiting what your heart secretly longs for. What unmet needs and desires make these books appealing to you?

WOMEN LONG TO ESCAPE REALITY

Many women get pulled into erotica simply because they are bored, desperate for an escape from the drudgery of normal life. There are seasons of life that can feel very routine, in which nothing new or challenging seems to happen. This often leaves women feeling lonely and depressed. They want to have a "pulse" again, dream again, and hope again. So, what's the harm in an imaginary story that takes you away from the drudgery of your life? If you can't have a real adventure, at least you can enjoy an imaginary one—one that's guaranteed to have a happy ending.

Erotica promises to take you out of your boring world and inject some adventure—even if it's only in your mind. For a brief time, you can feel alive imagining what it would be like to fall madly in love with a gorgeous man, to be so beautiful that heads always turn your way, to ride on a private jet to an ocean getaway, or to have mind-blowing orgasms at will.

The fact is: your heart *was* designed for adventure, intrigue, romance, and suspense. These are the things that make you feel alive. God made your body to physically respond with invigorating chemicals like adrenaline, dopamine, and cortisol when life becomes exciting and semi-unpredictable.

Your longing is legitimate. We just believe there are ways to get what you are looking for without compromising God's standards.

WOMEN LONG TO BE CHERISHED BY A MAN

My dating relationship with Mike began to take a serious turn. We were standing in my parents' driveway and he was giving me a good-night kiss, holding me in his arms. He looked up to the starry Florida sky and yelled, "God, I want this one!" At that moment, a thrill ran through my body. Out of all the women in the universe, Mike wanted me!

In every romance novel, erotic or otherwise, the female character longs for that experience of being chosen and cherished by the guy. Authors haven't invented this as a major theme of romance—their stories simply reflect what every woman deeply longs for in her heart.

One woman who has a physically disabled husband put it this way:

Reading *Fifty Shades of Grey* gave me a sense of hope in a way. I was able to feel the love the main character Christian felt and also feel the way the girl was so taken by him. I live a very harsh reality at thirty years old. I may never feel the love of my husband again, so if reading a book is a way I can vicariously live that life, then great. I am my husband's caregiver as well as taking care of two kids, not to mention all the home stuff. These books are approximately 500 +

pages each and I got through all three in the matter of four days. They kept my attention, and I honestly think there was some longing. I want that love!!!!!

Maybe you too remember being some man's "one and only" in the early years of marriage. Or maybe you're still waiting to be the one a man wants. Does your heart ache and long to be cherished?

WOMEN LONG TO BE PROTECTED BY A STRONG MAN

In a culture that constantly celebrates women's independence and freedom, do you find it strange that a book about bondage is spreading like wildfire? All of a sudden, words like "submission," "master," and "obedience" are not only acceptable but sexy. Even the most liberal women in the media are talking about the thrill of a strong man. In a conversation on *The View* about *Fifty Shades of Grey*, the fearless five—Whoopi Goldberg, Joy Behar, Elisabeth Hasselbeck, Sherri Shepherd, and Barbara Walters—were discussing *why* women loved the book so much. Barbara suggested that "when you go home, you want the guy to be in charge."[1]

This seems to have come out of left field. But it hasn't really. The mantra that "you don't need a man" has created a culture of strong women and weak men. No longer is it considered romantic or chivalrous for a man to open a door for his date or even to ask a woman out in the first place. Men have been told, "Step aside—we can take care of ourselves!"

Now we secretly yearn for the very thing our independence has destroyed—strong, confident men. There is something wonderful and even erotic about trusting the strength of a man who can provide, protect, and lead. So, women are caught at the crossroads of wanting the strength of a man, but not wanting to be controlled. We ask our husbands or boyfriends, "Why won't you lead?" Then, when they show strength, we respond with the feedback, "You can lead but not *that* way!"

Think about the movies you loved as a girl: *The Little Mermaid. The Princess Bride. Cinderella.* The more modern version found in *Ever After.* Think of Buttercup awaiting rescue from her simple farm boy in *The Princess Bride*: "My Westley will always come for me." And so, he did. And our hearts swoon, but we'd never say we want that in real life. Why? Because that might display weakness—something that's *not* in vogue for the modern woman!

In *Captivating*, author Stasi Eldredge broke down the conflict between wanting a strong man and being a woman molded by modern feminism. She wrote: "I simply loved feeling wanted and fought for. This desire is set deep in the heart of every little girl—and every woman. Yet most of us are ashamed of it. We downplay it. We pretend it is less than it is. We are women of the twenty-first century after all—strong, independent, and capable, thank you very much. Uh-huh . . . and who is buying all those romance novels?"[2]

Over 70 million women. That's who.

WOMEN LONG TO RESCUE A MAN

We are all familiar with relationships where the good girl believed she could tame the bad boy. Some women are consumed by the desire to rescue the man they love. In a strange way, they are more attracted to a troubled man who needs help than to a normal, uncomplicated "nice guy." They tolerate rude and even abusive behavior with the hope that "someday my love will change him."

The Fifty Shades series and many other erotica story lines play on this longing, making it a primary part of the plot. Christian, the main character in the novels, has everything. He's handsome, young, rich, talented, and successful. If the description of him stopped there, frankly he wouldn't be that interesting. The charm of his two-dimensional appeal would wear off like a Hollywood heartthrob on the cover of a magazine. But Christian becomes more appealing and intriguing because he's also very messed up. He has dark, mysterious wounds from his childhood that no psychologist can heal. He is deathly afraid of true intimacy, so he substitutes it with kinky sex. In short, he needs a woman to save him from himself. His internal imperfection adds the irresistible element to his outward perfection. He must be saved. Ana's heart is broken, thinking of Christian as a traumatized, abused little boy who has never known true love. Although she is at times concerned about her safety, how could she leave him alone? Ana goes beyond wanting to help him—she becomes his savior.

All of us have a deep, imbedded desire to make a profound difference in the life of a man. The desire to help the man you love is a worthy aspiration. In fact, it's biblical. God created you to be a completer or "helper" for the man you marry. How wonderful that God also gave you the innate longing to do just that. Like every healthy desire, this one also can be twisted and skewed, which is what led Kim into an abusive relationship:

> My senior year in college, a mutual friend introduced me to Dan. Dan was several years older than me, a committed Christian, and headed toward seminary to become a worship pastor. The attraction was immediate, and I thought I had found a man I could marry. But as our dating relationship progressed, Dan became controlling, jealous, and paranoid about my past relationships. He constantly questioned me about what I was thinking or why I was late, and often accused me of being unfaithful to him. The arguments and accusations escalated to screaming in my face, calling me names, and eventually grabbing me.
>
> Looking back, I wonder why I didn't just call it quits. I'm a strong-willed person, the last you would expect to find in an abusive relationship. But Dan had a troubled past: an abusive father and a history of drug abuse. I wanted to prove that I was trustworthy and that my unconditional love was strong enough to endure. I'm not a quitter. I wanted to see

the best in him and believed that with God's help he could change. Sadly, he did not.

There is nothing romantic about enabling an abusive man. It is yet another example of a beautiful longing twisted by evil. Yet the Fifty Shades series tiptoes right up to the line of proclaiming that a woman's love can save a man from his demons.

WOMEN LONG TO BE SEXUALLY ALIVE

And then there's the sex. Let's put it out there ... many, if not most, women long to have the kind of sex promised in the movies and on the cover of *Cosmo*. Maybe you aren't married yet but your sexual appetite is alive and well—and frustrated. Or perhaps you are married and have a husband whose sexual desire isn't quite as strong as yours. It could be that your sexuality represents deep wounds of childhood abuse. Being with a man feels very unsafe but you still long to be touched and loved.

No matter the sexual hardship you're facing, women are drawn to the promise of sexual fulfillment and the ability to fully surrender to it. You long to experience the deep pleasure and release that you've heard is supposed to be part of sex. But your normal, everyday life doesn't provide that. Enter erotica. No man needed, no risks of heartbreak involved, you don't even have to put on makeup ... just start reading and you can have your body and mind awakened any time you want.

Sexually charged books seem a lot less harmful than having a bunch of "hookups," cheating on your husband, or looking at pornographic images on the Internet. Maybe you consider them to be an acceptable outlet for you as a single woman. Or maybe, as many women claim, books like the Fifty Shades books can wake up your libido, helping you to become the lover you want to be to your husband.

We want to be very clear: your sexual desire is not wrong. God created you to be sexual. Your body and your mind are wired to long for sexual pleasure and intimacy. Unfortunately, many religious messages separate being a sexual woman from being a spiritual woman. Instead of encouraging you to seek God's plan for your sexuality, you're left with only worldly outlets to fulfill your longings.

Whether you are single or married, sexually dead or frustrated, we will address your desire to be a sexual *and* spiritual woman in this book. You don't have to turn off your desire to know God in order to turn on your desire to be sexual.

A SECRET LONGING

There is no shame in these longings.

In fact, we cannot ignore them, keeping them tucked away in the darkest corners of our hearts. Satan has power in secrets and in darkness, but his power dissipates when we bring our desires and struggles into the light to talk about them and yield them to God.

My single friend Rita makes no bones about the fact that she'd like someone to cuddle, have dinner with, laugh with, and to carry the burden of financial decisions. At fifty years old, she talks openly about hoping to have sex one day. And yet, she's really happy. I asked her one day how she could want a husband so much and yet be one of the most joyful and content women that I know. She says the key is being fully aware of her longings and to do the hard work of finding safe places to talk about them and examine them in the light of what Jesus says.

Sadly, many women don't feel safe to admit that they are lonely, bored, or sexually frustrated. Thinking that "Christian women should have this under control," they bury these longings, and that's where the danger arises. Things like erotica, porn, and affairs call to us when we ignore our longings. That's what happened to Susie.

Susie is a spiritual woman. She and her husband are both church and community leaders and have chosen to home-school their children. About the time *Fifty Shades of Grey* was released, she was experiencing a frustration with the reality of waking up to the hard work of schooling every day. She was bored with her life and began to seek excitement through sexual temptation. Due to her leadership positions, she didn't feel she could tell anyone what she was struggling with, and instead found a solution in reading erotica. She wrote this to us:

> I cannot tell you how much I love my children. I have always wanted to be a wife and mother—more than any career life could offer. But I began to feel like my life was boring and mundane. I was struggling and

thought I needed something exciting. To be blunt, *my husband doesn't have a sexual appetite that matches mine*. Don't get me wrong—I am very satisfied by my husband when we do have sex—but he doesn't need touch and could go a week probably without even thinking of kissing me. I get sad and lonely.

I read *Fifty Shades* three times . . . this opened the window of curiosity to many other books like these. I spent hours in the evenings reading those books. As soon as I could, I would escape to my reading spot. I told myself that I needed an *escape from reality*.

I became unsatisfied with everything in life. I became more unsatisfied in our marriage. I was not satisfied by [my husband] sexually during that time period. It was horrible. He couldn't satisfy me—and it was my fault.

I had thoughts of packing my bags and living a different life.

Susie didn't get what she was longing for when she turned to erotica. Fifty Shades tapped into her desire to escape her ordinary life and to feel sexually alive. Instead of finding herself sexually alive and escaping her reality, she was less sexually satisfied and almost left the good and treasured reality of being a wife and a mom. She was deceived.

We know you have longings—we have them too! This book is not just about helping you understand why you read the Fifty Shades series (or may want to read it). We want to point you to healthy ways of addressing and meeting your longings. Too many women like Susie have been tricked into believing that an erotic book or online relationship can fulfill their deep needs. It's time to expose that trap and reveal a way that leads to life.

Pull Back the Shades

It's time to let the light shine into the room of your heart that contains your deepest longings. Using the list of the five longings on page 17, determine which of these are unmet in your life and may be leaving you open to acting out with erotica, porn, or in other ways. You might even write a letter to God expressing your frustration for the unmet longings in your life. It's good to get it out!

Chapter 2

Fifty Shades of Deception

My favorite movie is *You've Got Mail*. A woman's online world meets real life. The romance of Kathleen Kelly (Meg Ryan) and "NY152"—the screen name by which she knows her pursuer, is built strictly upon the nonpersonal interface of email. Her mind creates and perfects him, using only the words they share in emails. She doesn't realize that she's already met him in real life. He is Joe Fox (Tom Hanks), someone she really deserves to hate and whose imperfections could never make way for love. Or could they? He carefully "tweaks" their real-life relationship one encounter at a time in hopes that he can win her heart.

In the last scene of the movie, Kathleen finally schedules a chance to "meet" NY152 at Riverside Park in Manhattan. When she sees Joe, she realizes that her dream is becoming an imperfectly wonderful reality with a man she already knows. Through tears she says to him: "I wanted it to be you. I wanted it to be you so badly."

Want to know what's even more romantic than that fictional scene? One created ten years later in the same park. For our twentieth anniversary, Bob rescued me from my reality of deadlines, car pool, and grocery shopping, and he re-created the romance of the movie, taking me to each location in New York City where Kathleen and Joe slowly fell in love. We ended in Riverside Park where he told me that after twenty years, he still wanted it to be me. (Now if I could only get him to pick up his socks!) I know that story sounds awfully picture-perfect. I assure you we are full of flaws and I will share them later in the book, but, every now and then, my man hits a home run in the game of romance!

Women love a great romantic escape, but be careful how you escape, because some fiction or online relationships promise to satisfy, but in the end they lead to more dissatisfaction. We have met with women who started reading erotica to awaken their sex lives with their husbands, but it actually caused them to be less satisfied in their marriage bed than ever. Single women have told us they used porn as a "sexual outlet until marriage" but it suffocated their desire to pursue a relationship at all. And we have counseled hearts wounded deeply by online relationships gone bad. What seemed innocent to them ended up being harmful.

How is a woman to know when a romantic escape is dangerous?

DISCERNING THE DANGER OF FANTASY

Having read the Fifty Shades trilogy, I will say with great confidence that these books are not merely fiction—a story that *could* be true but is not—but are actually *fantasy*—something that could *not* possibly be true. Erotica like Fifty Shades is fantasy because it subtly asks you to assume a different reality. It can be entertaining to enter a fantasy and imagine a visit a realm that can't possibly be true (The Lord of the Rings series comes to mind). So, when does fantasy present dangerous deception? Should we avoid all books and movies that are not grounded solidly in reality?

Here are two questions that will help you decide for yourself whether or not fantasy, or any other form of fiction, presents a dangerous deception: What laws are changed? And what does it inspire?

What laws are changed?

One of the most widely known fantasy stories starts out like this: "A long time ago, in a galaxy far, far away . . ." From the outset, the author of *Star Wars* is asking you to step away from what you know to be true and imagine with him a different galaxy, a different time, with different assumptions. The story is filled with creatures like Wookiees and talking robots, time warps and space travel. We accept these illogical elements because we know they are part of fantasy.

Erotica also lures you into a different reality but doesn't let you know that you are entering a world "far, far away." Within the context of "normal life," erotica introduces romantic stories that are not possible. But what makes erotica unrealistic is far more subtle and yet more dangerous. *Instead of manipulating laws of physics and science, erotica authors like EL James change moral and relational laws.* Right and wrong get morphed into a morally grey universe that becomes impossible to untwist. While reading *Fifty Shades of Grey*, I emailed a friend, stating, "I can no longer find true north!" I got sucked into the fantasy. EL James states that redefining morality was part of her agenda in writing the books. In one interview she said, "What I wanted to demonstrate is that I do not look at the world in terms of black and white—and I find people who do rather scary. I think it's all shades of grey."[3] Fantasy becomes very dangerous when an author takes creative license to alter moral and spiritual truth.

Just as there are scientific laws in our universe—such as gravity—there are also principles that govern our emotions, relationships, and spiritual health. You have freedom to choose if you will abide by them, but you can never be free from the consequences of your actions. For instance, if you eat chocolate cake and potato chips all day every day, your body will not function as it should. If you jump out of a second story window, you will break a few bones at best. When you violate physical, moral, or spiritual laws, you will eventually have to live with the consequences.

Erotica twists and distorts the results of making immoral and foolish choices. In the real world, our actions have consequences, sometimes very grave consequences. The authors of erotica simply ignore or erase those consequences and create a magical "happy ending." Solomon warns against falling into this delusional thinking. After talking about the dangers of sexual immorality, he writes, "Can a man (or woman) scoop fire into his lap without his clothes being burned? Can a man walk on hot coals without his feet being scorched?" (Proverbs 6:27–28).

Here's a reality check: you cannot pursue the kinds of relationships you read about in erotica without an outcome very different from the ones in the books. If you read Fifty Shades and then invest in a relationship that is built around sexual sadism, you will *not* end up in a loving, caring, committed marriage.

This is what happened to a young missionary and Christian leader:

I am single and erotica has ruined my life. I have been addicted for ten years and I am only twenty-five.

No one knows my struggle. No one knows that I have lived an isolated life because I have found more solace in fantasies aroused in my mind by erotica than in real relationships.

Erotica seems harmless because it's just words on a page but it brands your mind, creates false expectations for future relationships. I can't even maintain real relationships because I feel like a shallow pretender hiding one of the biggest parts of my life.

Erotica perpetuated my "need" for meeting people online because I didn't know how to develop or maintain relationships with people outside of the screen. Eventually, I decided to take my online relationships into reality. Many of the stories I read portrayed rape or power-struggle situations as exciting. A no didn't always mean no because, in the end, the girl always seemed to end up just fine. So when I met one of my first guys offline, I was thrust ever too quickly into a scenario I had read about but, unlike the stories, I didn't end up fine. My no didn't mean no, and I was sexually abused by a man who did the same things to me that I had read about in those erotic stories. But in my story, there wasn't a happy ending.

Ever since then, I have carried the weight of shame and guilt from putting myself into that situation six years ago. Erotica makes it seem normal for us to be used and abused, but it's not normal.

Be careful little eyes what you read. You cannot change emotional, relational, and spiritual laws in real life, but erotica may lead you to believe that you can.

What does it inspire?

Even though fantasy by definition takes us out of some aspect of reality, it can use imagination to point us to deeper truth. For example, C. S. Lewis's book series The Chronicles of Narnia takes great license in creating a fantasy in which a magical wardrobe transports children into the world of Narnia. There is a white witch, half human-half animal creatures, and a mighty lion who is so self-sacrificing that some have suggested he is a Christ-figure. While Lewis changes the laws of nature, he is drawing attention to deeper spiritual truths about the captivity we live in, Jesus' sacrifice to free us from sin and God's final victory over evil.

The Hunger Games is another example of fantasy intended to point out a truth even while bending reality. Whether or not you like the books or movies, they cause you to think about how we categorize and "cannibalize" each other to survive and maintain power.

What is erotica intended to inspire? Rather than pointing to a deeper truth, erotica uses fantasy ultimately to promote deception—to make you believe that you can have everything you've ever longed for. Let's take a logical look at the absurdity of what is presented in the Fifty Shades of Grey series.

By the end of the second book, Christian and Ana have known each other for six weeks. They are engaged and madly in love. Christian is a multibillionaire (he makes $100,000 an hour!) at the age of twenty-seven. This self-made man has all the time and money in the world to dote on his new love. During their courtship, they've had some amazing dates, including rides in his private helicopter, gliding, and a day on his personal yacht. And he has given Anastasia:

- a Blackberry
- an iPad
- a mac laptop
- a new wardrobe
- a book collection worth $14,000
- a brand-new Saab convertible
- a house on the coast of Seattle
- and, a personal trainer

He also bought the company she works for so he can keep an eye on her.

Is it possible for a young man to be so wealthy? Sure. There are a few Bill Gateses and Mark Zuckerbergs out there who could potentially buy a woman everything she ever wanted. But let's add to the money the fact that Christian is incredibly fit and handsome and always knows exactly what to say and do to win Ana's heart. He is controlling, but apparently not smothering. He is angry and aggressive, but somehow not abusive. Such a man does not exist! Both how he behaves and how she reacts to his behavior are pure fantasy—of the most deceptive kind.

And the sex . . . let's just say it reaches the outer-limit of fantasy. This couple does it everywhere, every way, all the time. They both are always ready for sex and quickly reach orgasm time and time again and at the same moment. They instantly know how to please each other, always have the energy, and their bodies magically respond to each other's touch. Every argument they have can be dissolved by great sex. They can be furious with each other but one sexual touch instantly makes it all right again. And to top it off, as is the case with most fictional sex, there is never a mess involved.

Does this sound like your reality?

❖　❖　❖

The fantasy of erotica inspires one thing—the longing for more. Instead of satisfying your longings, it will awaken,

36

manipulate, and deepen them. No longer will you be satisfied with an attentive boyfriend or husband who occasionally brings you a soy latte to cheer you up . . . you will want a man who is obsessively, unrealistically in love with you and has the bank account to prove it. Normal sex in your marriage—the kind that requires communication, sometimes involves frustration, and doesn't always end in rapturous orgasm—will now be disappointing. A hardworking man who is faithfully scraping by will never be able to provide for you the way a man in your fantasy can.

And it's not always the harder erotica fantasies like Fifty Shades that create the deception. We know of a single woman who has feasted so obsessively on Christian romance novels that no man can live up to her expectations. She remains addicted to the fiction and is unable to experience authentic relationships in her real world. The end result of living in fantasy is disillusionment, dissatisfaction, and ungratefulness in reality. If you desperately desire to have a fulfilling love life, to be alive and satisfied, erotica will not get you there. You will never reach contentment reading something that is intended to make you long for more!

You may be thinking, "I can tell the difference between truth and fiction. I'm not the type of woman to get pulled in." We talk to many women who cannot see their own deception even as they were buried in the emotional, relational, and spiritual consequences of the lies that have destroyed them. That's the hard part: by their very nature, lies are deceptive, not easily detected. The thought that you are not vulnerable to deception is evidence that you are. Paul has a warning for that kind of thinking: "If you think you are standing firm, be careful that you don't fall!" (1 Corinthians 10:12).

When Bob and I were first married, it seemed that even the slightest hint of romance or sex in a movie or book or song invited me into a fantasy world. Though I don't remember having any overtly sexual fantasies, I was a master at creating a perfect man in my mind. Usually Bob was the man, but oh how "perfected" he was in my fantasy. All the dreaming in the world didn't turn him into that man. In fact, it was driving me away from him.

We have learned that our own hearts are deceptive and we are vulnerable to the deception of the enemy. It is only by constant dependence on God's truth that we can stand because so often Satan's deception looks so inviting. The Bible tells us that Satan poses as an "angel of light" (2 Corinthians 11:14). He is so motivated to see us believe untruth that he's even willing to look like he belongs to God when that is the very thing he hates.

Why? Is it just to see us addicted to erotica, overwhelmed by lust, void of true love, and living in the ruin of broken relationships? No, those are just symptoms of the ultimate goal in his plan to deceive us. What he is after is much bigger than you or me. In the next chapter, we'd like to reveal to you Satan's real agenda.

Pull Back the Shades

The Bible says that Satan is "a liar and the father of lies" (John 8:44). What lies have you believed about your longings? And what consequences have you faced as a result? Consider this prayerfully so that God opens your eyes to see any deception of which you may not be aware.

Chapter 3

Why Mommy Porn Is Spiritual

When the current wave of erotica hit us, the term "mommy porn" came with it. But it's not just moms reading porn crafted with black-and-white words. It's their daughters, too. The youngest reader of erotica who corresponded with us as we wrote this book began when she was *nine*. But many were in their tweens or teens when they began. Here's what eighteen-year-old Shelli tells us:

> I stumbled upon porn when I was about twelve, and I quickly became obsessed with it due to a sort of morbid curiosity. I was pretty much addicted. I read online erotica too.

Shelli reported feelings of guilt for using porn and erotica when she was younger. She was careful to hide her use from her "conservative Christian" parents. But then she found a mentor who she thought "helped her a lot," but something worse happened. See if you can follow her logic here:

> Now . . . my view has completely changed. I realized that hating myself and thinking I was disgusting was

actually really bad for me! And then I realized that not understanding my own sexuality and thinking that it exists only for one man was a form of misogyny! I started reading up on gender studies, on female sexuality, and on human sexuality in general. Because I'm not so obsessed with "purity" now, I no longer have to have a dark obsession with sex.

My heart is broken for Shelli. In her quest to find freedom, she has been misguided into another lie. Her conclusion that to pursue purity and to believe that God created her to have sex with one man is misogyny—that is, the idea of having sex with one man portrays hatred toward women—is a very dark line of thinking. Though she never intended to arrive at this place, I believe the Enemy of her soul had that on the agenda from the very beginning. What designs does the Enemy have on you?

AN EPIC BATTLE

Do you believe there are forces of good and evil in the world—that humans are constantly in the crosshairs of an epic battle that can only be described as spiritual? Juli and I do. And we think most of the world does. Just look at the popular literature of our culture—even children's stories are filled with good guys and bad guys. Forces for good and forces for evil. The plots around *Star Wars, Avatar, The Wizard of Oz, Sleeping Beauty, Harry Potter, The Lord of the Rings,* and *Twilight* have little else in common other than they suggest a spiritual struggle.

Through the Bible, we can discover and discern the two leading forces of good and evil in this epic battle. The Lord God Almighty is our Creator and the source of everything pure, holy, and redemptive. He is good. Satan is a powerful fallen angel who rebelled against God. He and his demons are in constant battle against God. He is evil (Isaiah 14:12–15).

But where are the battle lines drawn? Is a "good witch" who uses "white magic" on the side of good or a deceptive expression of darkness? Can a vampire—a symbol of death—become a symbol of life and love if he is "good"? Could erotica become good if it awakens a dead sexual life, or is it an outlet for the single woman who is struggling to be pure? Be careful before you answer any of these questions. One of Satan's strategies is to confuse the battle lines. As we mentioned in the last chapter, "Satan himself masquerades as an angel of light" (2 Corinthians 11:14). He is crafty, deceptive, and even attractive. He often uses your very legitimate but unmet longings to seduce you into destruction.

❖   ❖   ❖

With this in mind, let's consider mommy porn. I believe this genre of literature and Fifty Shades books specifically are very spiritual books with an aggressive spiritual agenda. Reading mommy porn is not just a little guilty pleasure. It doesn't simply represent a love story with some kinky sex scenes. It takes you on a wild emotional and sexual ride. But unlike an exciting roller coaster, you will not be dropped off right back where you started. These books take you on a journey that has a spiritual impact and an intended spiritual destination: destruction.

MOMMY PORN DISTORTS SEX

The definition of erotica is "art or literature intended to arouse sexual desire." Why is this a spiritual issue? Because sex is inherently spiritual.

God designed sex as a powerful symbol and celebration of covenant love. It is a physical and emotional expression of the deepest commitment two people can make to each other. But sex is more than that. It represents the ultimate covenant love—God's love for His people.

The Bible constantly uses language related to marriage and sexual intimacy to express aspects of our relationship with God. The New Testament tells us we are the bride, He is the groom. Worshiping an idol is referred to as adultery and prostitution. Old Testament prophets often spoke of Israel as God's bride and even use sexual terms to describe the intimacy He desired with His people. The Hebrew word for sexual intimacy, *yada*, means "to know, to be known, to be deeply respected." It is a word that transcended the physical act to speak of a deep emotional connection. In a beautiful expression of His desire to know us, God inspired that this same word be used in the Scriptures to express a deep knowing and longing for God. "You have searched me, Lord, and you know (*yada*) me" (Psalm 139:1).

Because sex is a portrait of God's sacred love, Satan will

do anything he can to destroy the beauty of it. He has tried to twist, tarnish, and distort the beautiful and holy picture of sexuality in every way possible. From creating shame about sexuality in Christian women to sexual abuse and prostitution, his agenda is to separate us from ever celebrating sexuality within the context of God's holy design. Sex has been dragged through the mud so thoroughly that most people can't even comprehend that it is intended to be something holy. Sex trafficking, pornography, friends with benefits, sexual perversions and addictions—they all paint an animalistic and degrading picture of something that was created to be a glorious expression of human and divine love.

Reading mommy porn is falling right into this spiritual agenda.

Evil's primary attack on sexuality is to simplify it—to separate the physical act of sex from human love and divine design. Every time sex is abused or distorted, the physical act is split off from the relational and spiritual elements of sex. If you have suffered through sexual abuse, your body may have been aroused by how you were being fondled. Yet your heart was crying out, "I don't want this!" You were physically aroused while being spiritually and emotionally violated. In a hookup relationship, you may have felt physical pleasure and even a moment of being loved, but it was quickly replaced by shame and rejection when you each moved on to the next hookup partner.

Erotica like Fifty Shades of Grey is aimed at awakening your physical sexual desire without any connection to emotional, relational, or spiritual reality. Even if the main characters are "in love," you are not! Whatever emotional and sexual response these novels create in you, they are disconnected from your love relationships and your longing to know and honor God.

Reading erotica, like viewing pornography, may lead to an intense sexual reaction but the characters are one-dimensional lies. With each page of erotica or image of porn on a computer, evil is reinforcing the lie that sex is just about physical pleasure—divorced from true commitment, unselfish love, and God's holy design. You will be left with a deep ache for something more. The truth is you were created for something more! Your sexuality was never meant to be separate from your deepest spiritual and relational longings but to be an expression of them.

IS NOTHING HOLY?

As mentioned earlier, I read all three of the books in the Fifty Shades series. The explicit scenes bothered me, but what haunted me even more was the seemingly intentional agenda to drag God and His holiness into the sewer. Most people who read these books seem to be so mesmerized by the sexuality that they appear to walk right past what I perceive as an even greater danger and offense: spiritual darkness. In fact, those who haven't read this particular series need to know that what I write ahead is definitely graphic, but I feel so strongly about this terrible offense that I have to sound an alarm.

I can't apply this to all mommy porn because I haven't read it, but Fifty Shades has plenty of spiritual language, including the name of the main character: Christian. The books are filled with Christian metaphors and allusions like, "I'm Eve in the Garden of Eden, and he's the serpent, and I cannot resist."[4] In the Red Room of Pain is an old wooden cross. At one point, Christian and Ana have sex with her pushed against the cross.

The author of Fifty Shades has two words that she obviously really likes because of how often she uses them throughout the books. The first word is profane—the "F-word." It is used in some form approximately one hundred times in each of the three books. Surprisingly, her other favorite word is *holy*, which is also used approximately one hundred times in each book. Whenever the word *holy* is used, it is paired with another word. Here are some of the combinations:

- Holy crap
- Holy hell
- Holy s***
- Holy f***
- Holy Moses
- Holy mother f*****

Before you think I'm splitting hairs, making a big deal out of nothing, consider that the word *holy* means to be set apart or consecrated unto God. The third person of the Trinity bears the name "Holy Spirit." There are few words that are more central to the description and expression of who God is. The few times in the Bible we get a glimpse of someone actually standing in the presence of God, holiness is always central to that experience.

- When Moses encountered God in the burning bush, he was told to remove his shoes because he is standing on "holy ground" (Exodus 3:5).
- The place where God lived among the Israelites was called the "holy of holies."
- The prophet Isaiah was ushered into the heavenly temple of God. Above the Lord were seraphs (angels), each with six wings, covering their faces as they sang: "Holy, holy, holy is the Lord Almighty; the whole earth is full of his glory" (Isaiah 6:3).
- John wrote the book of Revelation to record the spectacular visions of the future the Lord showed him. In Revelation 4, John records that he stood before God's throne in heaven. Creatures surround the throne; day and night they never stop declaring: "*Holy, holy, holy is the Lord God Almighty, who was, and is, and is to come*" (Revelation 4:8).

Holy is a word that describes the indescribable and causes us to worship One who is pure and perfect in power. That the word *holy* would be used casually is one thing. But to link it with the filth of sin and evil is an appalling offense to our God.

One more example of how the holy is profaned is particularly disturbing. While in the Red Room of Pain, Christian has bound Anastasia's hands and feet spread-eagle to the bed, blindfolded her, and is erotically flogging her. The spiritual aspects of the scene are obvious based on the conversation surrounding the action. Here are a few of things Anastasia says:

> . . . *seven shades of sin in one enticing look. My mouth dries, and I know I will do anything he asks.*[5]

> . . . *he sounds like the devil himself.*[6]

> *I am dragged into a dark, dark part of my psyche that surrenders to this most erotic sensation . . . I've entered a very dark, carnal place.*[7]

During this whole episode, Christian has music blaring into Anastasia's ears. She describes the music as "a celestial choir—singing a capella in my head, an ancient, ancient hymnal. *What in heaven's name is this?*"[8] The ancient Latin hymn sung during this carnal bondage and fornication is called "Spem in Alium." Here are the words translated into English:

> I have never put my hope in any other but in You,
> O God of Israel
> who can show both anger

and graciousness,
and who absolves all the sins of suffering man
Lord God,
Creator of Heaven and Earth
be mindful of our lowliness.

I doubt that EL James intentionally included these spiritual, holy themes in order to aggravate Christians. However, I am absolutely convinced that Satan, through these books, intended to mock and desecrate things set apart to worship God. When I have talked to Christians who have read *Fifty Shades of Grey*, they are quick to admit the sexual themes in the book, but none of them mention or even seem to notice these more subtle offenses to our faith. Yet I believe this is the more direct and belligerent attack. If you call yourself by the name "Christian," identifying yourself as a "Christ-follower," I beg you to allow the full impact of that offense hit you: defend the name and character of our God!

MOMMY PORN MAKES AN IDOL OF LOVE

Do you remember the Ten Commandments? Some of them are quite straightforward and understandable such as: don't murder, covet, steal, or lie. But the first two commandments are more difficult to apply to our lives. Here they are:

You shall have no other gods before me.
You shall not make for yourself an image in the form of anything in heaven above or on the earth beneath

50

or in the waters below. You shall not bow down to them or worship them; for I, the Lord your God, am a jealous God. (Deuteronomy 5:7–9)

When you read these commandments, your mind might visualize statues and barbaric customs of bowing down to a "bird god" or worshiping the stars. This certainly doesn't seem to be a temptation in our day. Not so fast. These first two commandments are ultimately about worship.

Every culture promotes idols—things or ideas that take the place of God in our lives. One of the primary gods of Western culture is the god of love. In ancient times, she was a Greek goddess named Aphrodite and he was a Roman god named Venus. Today, we are too sophisticated to invent names for what we worship, yet we continue to worship love.

"Love is an idol? Seriously? Aren't you taking this a little too far?" you might protest. "After all, isn't love a good thing? Doesn't the Bible teach about how important love and marriage are?" Absolutely! I'm all for love and marriage. My whole ministry is devoted to helping women restore their marriages and grow in love. But a *good* thing that becomes the *primary* thing immediately becomes an *immoral* thing. Any good gift from God that is exalted above God becomes a tool of the enemy. Love, sex, and marriage are prime candidates.

Tim Keller defines an idol as "anything more important to you than God, anything that absorbs your heart and imagination more than God, anything you seek to give you what only God can give. [It] is anything so central and essential to your life that, should you lose it, your life would feel hardly worth living. . . . An idol is whatever you look at and say in your heart of hearts, 'If I have that, then I'll feel my life has meaning, then I'll know I have value, then I'll feel significant and secure.'"[9]

Erotica writers overtly present romantic love and great sex as the salvation of a forlorn woman. And who can blame them? If there is no God, what better replacement than a handsome, strong, loving, sexy man?

As Keller writes, "We maintain the fantasy that if we find our one true soul mate, everything wrong with us will be healed . . . the love object is God."[10] This is a primary theme in all erotica and certainly dominates Fifty Shades. Ana becomes a savior to Christian, her love erasing all the pain of his past and healing him. Christian's psychologist tells her, "I don't mean to stress how important a role you have in his Damascene conversion—his road to Damascus. But you have."[11] The "saving" isn't one-sided. Ana is equally attached to Christian: "Oh, I love him so. I will be nothing without him, nothing but a shadow—all the light eclipsed."[12]

At one level, this kind of love and devotion is beautiful and endearing. But it is also very dangerous. No man, no amount of great sex—even the best marriage—can ever and should ever take the place of God.

Satan's ultimate agenda is not just to get you to sin but to keep you from worshiping God. He will use anything—good or bad—to accomplish that purpose. Whether you are addicted to crack cocaine or addicted to the love of a fantasy man makes no difference. They both keep you enslaved to something that has replaced God.

A VERY REAL IMPACT

There are consequences when we choose to worship something other than God. Many women have written to us to share the very real spiritual impact of erotica in their lives. The stakes are very high. Here's the destruction one woman experienced:

> At the peak of my addiction, I was spending five to six hours a day watching porn (both free and paid sites) and reading [erotica]. I was a high school small group leader, active in my church, and all the while dying on the inside. I started drinking, abusing Ambien, and ended up on depression medicine. Suicide was a real thought.

This is not a surprising destination for someone who embraces the lies of the enemy. Jesus makes the outcome of the spiritual battle very clear. He said, "The thief comes only to steal and kill and destroy; I have come that they may have life, and have it to the full" (John 10:10). Do you want destruction? Run toward the enemy with your longings and brace yourself for relational dysfunction, depression, and an increase in your unmet longings, among other things. If you cooperate with him by reading erotica, you will face his destructiveness.

I think it's important to note that not every woman will end up addicted or with lives that are completely destroyed—but all spiritual women will feel consequences at some level. One woman wrote:

> The Holy Spirit convicted me when I first started [reading erotica]. I ignored Him. After a while, I no longer heard Him. I didn't even want to be at church. I missed God. I missed our relationship. But the deeper I got—the more I felt like I needed to run from Him and not to Him.

That's kind of the whole point of this chapter: Are you running from God or toward Him? We believe you have a choice to make.

It's certainly not fun or politically correct for Juli and me to confront you in this way. But that is exactly what Jesus did. He told the religious leaders that their father was Satan because they didn't believe Him (John 8:43–47). He told one of His closest friends, "Get behind me, Satan! You are thinking of the things of men, not the things of God" (Matthew 16:23, my paraphrase). Ouch!

Maybe you've found yourself on the wrong side of the spiritual battle. Please remember Jesus' words when He walked the earth. His words to you are not about condemnation but an invitation. He is inviting you and me to say no to the world's distortions and say yes to the true love story. The question is, What will you choose today? There is no middle ground.

But you do have a choice. It's not too late. The Giver of Life offers it to you no matter how deep you have fallen.

Pull Back the Shades

When you let the light seep in, you'll recognize there is a deep spiritual dynamic involved in the choices you make. The love stories of erotica are fictional, fantasy, an illusion. However, the spiritual agenda and its impact are real. Joshua reminded us, "If serving the Lord seems undesirable to you, then choose for yourselves this day whom you will serve . . . But as for me and my household, we will serve the Lord" (Joshua 24:15). Write a prayer of commitment to clearly verbalize your desire to choose to serve the Lord.

"The thief comes only to steal and kill and destroy; I have come that they may have life, and have it to the full."

—JOHN 10:10

Chapter 4

Some Things Really Are Black and White

Dear Mr. Grey,

You wanted to know why I felt confused after you . . . spanked, punished, beat, assaulted me. Well, during the whole alarming process, I felt demeaned, debased, and abused. And much to my mortification, you're right, I was aroused . . . What really worried me was how I felt afterward. And that's more difficult to articulate. I was happy that you were happy. I felt relieved that it wasn't as painful as I thought it would be. And when I was lying in your arms, I felt . . . sated. But I feel very uncomfortable, guilty even, feeling that way. It doesn't sit well with me, and I'm confused as a result.

Ana

Miss Steele,

I am grateful for your inexperience. I value it, and I'm only beginning to understand what it means. Simply put . . . it means that you are mine in every way. Yes, you were aroused, which in turn was very arousing, there's nothing wrong with that . . . **Don't waste your energy on guilt, feelings of wrongdoing, etc.** *We are consenting adults and what we do behind closed doors* *is between ourselves. You need to free your mind and listen to your body.*

Christian Grey[13]

In *Fifty Shades of Grey*, Ana has questions about what's right and what's wrong in the bedroom (Who doesn't?). Christian challenges her to listen to her body, not her mind, and erases the notion that some things are wrong. This erasing of right and wrong is undeniably one purpose of EL James when she wrote the series. Here's the longer version of a quote we shared with you earlier:

> What I wanted to demonstrate is that I do not look at the world in terms of black and white—and I find people who do rather scary. I think it's all shades of grey. As you read through the novel, you think, "Was she good? Was she bad? What was he saying? What went on?" And I think all of the questions that the story raises are not questions for me to answer. They are for the readers to decide for themselves—how they feel about everything.[14]

She is right. It is not her place to answer our questions about what's right or wrong in our bedrooms. So, whose place is it? Do we make moral decisions based on how we "feel about everything" or based on a standard of right and wrong?

We know women have lots of questions about sex. Questions like:

- Is oral sex okay? What about anal sex?
- Is it wrong to role-play with my husband?
- My husband likes to spank me. Is that okay?
- Do you think sex toys are wrong?
- What's wrong with a married couple watching porn together?

Single women have different questions, such as:

- Is masturbation okay?
- Is oral sex really sex?
- How far is too far?

The opinions on these questions will be as varied as the women you ask. We admit: it can be confusing. Some things are black and white, while others truly appear to be grey. While we might agree that sex outside of marriage is wrong, we give ourselves wiggle room. What if your needs aren't met by your husband? What if you're fifty and still not married? What if the relationship you're having with a married man is more emotional than physical? What if you've outgrown your marriage and this new relationship is a better fit? Although it might be "technically wrong," surely God understands and would make an exception.

Wouldn't He?

In the last chapter, we challenged you to think of your choices in light of a spiritual battle. If you have chosen God's plan for your life, go to the source of God's Word to unearth *His* truth on all your questions about sex. We want to help you do that in this chapter because, when it comes to sex, answers aren't always easy to discern. Let's try to figure out what's black and white and even admit that some things can be shades of grey.

SO WHAT *IS* BLACK AND WHITE?

If you want to know how to live by God's standard of morality, you have to know what He says about right and wrong in His Word. Sometimes the answers to moral questions aren't found in a chapter or verse, and sometimes things can seem pretty "grey." But constantly using the Bible as a reference guide for decisions will make you wise in discerning good from evil (Hebrews 5:14). There are three questions that can help you, as a single or married person, discern whether something is right or wrong.

Does God clearly say no?

There are some things the Bible is very clear about—particularly related to sex. Adultery, for example, is something God forbids. You cannot have sex with someone else's spouse. Here is a list of sexual acts that God forbids. It was compiled by a friend and theologian, Dr. Joseph Dillow. The things on it probably won't surprise you, but be warned: this is not a politically correct list. It's simply a compilation of God's boundaries concerning sex.

1. **Fornication:** Fornication is immoral sex. It comes from the Greek word *porneia* that means "unclean." This broad term includes sexual intercourse outside of marriage (1 Corinthians 7:2; 1 Thessalonians 4:3), sleeping with your stepmother (1 Corinthians 5:1), sex with a prostitute (1 Corinthians 6:15), and adultery (Matthew 5:32).

2. **Adultery:** Adultery, or sex with someone who is not your spouse, is a sin and was punishable in the Old Testament by death (Leviticus 20:10). In the New Testament, Jesus expanded adultery to mean not just physical acts but emotional acts in the mind and heart (Matthew 5:28).

3. **Homosexual relations:** The Bible is very clear that for a man to have sex with a man or a woman to have sex with a woman is detestable to God (Leviticus 18:22; 20:13; Romans 1:27; 1 Corinthians 6:9).

4. **Impurity:** There are several Greek words that are translated as "impurity." To become "impure" (Greek, *molyno*) can mean to lose one's virginity or to become defiled due to living out a secular and essentially pagan lifestyle (1 Corinthians 6:9; 2 Corinthians 7:1). The Greek word *rupos* often refers to moral uncleanness in general (Revelation 22:11).

5. **Orgies:** For a married couple to become involved in sex orgies with different couples is an obvious violation of sexual acts 1, 2, and 4.

6. **Prostitution:** Prostitution, which is paying for sex, is morally wrong and condemned throughout Scripture (Leviticus 19:29; Deuteronomy 23:17; Proverbs 7:4–27).

7. **Lustful passions:** First, let me tell you what this does *not* mean. Lustful passion does *not* refer to the powerful, God-given sexual desire for each other enjoyed by a married man and woman. Instead, it refers to an unrestrained, indiscriminate sexual desire for men or women other than the person's marriage partner (Mark 7:21–22; Ephesians 4:19).

8. **Sodomy:** In the Old Testament, sodomy refers to men lying with men. The English word means male homosexual intercourse or intercourse with animals. Unfortunately, some Christian teachers have erroneously equated sodomy with oral sex. This is not the way the term is used in the Bible. The sodomites in the Bible were male homosexuals, or temple prostitutes (both male and female).

9. **Obscenity and coarse jokes:** In Ephesians 4:29, Paul says, "Do not let any unwholesome talk come out of your mouths." The Greek word is very descriptive and literally means *rotten* or *decaying*. We have all been around people who can see a sexual connotation in some innocent phrase and then begin to snicker or

laugh. This is wrong. However, this does not rule out sexual humor in the privacy of marriage, but rather inappropriate sexual comments in a public setting.

10. **Incest:** Incest, or sex with family members or relatives, is specifically forbidden in Scripture (Leviticus 18:7–18; 20:11–21).[15]

If you find yourself wondering if something is okay with God, first ask: Is it on this list? If God has clearly said no, it is wrong.

Is it only between you and your husband?

Well, this question seems like a pretty obvious one. God said no to having sex outside of marriage and having sex with someone you're not married to. So why do we even ask this question? Because many people fudge on it—and erotica is a perfect example.

Reserving sex, sexual fantasies, and sexual expression only for your husband means more than just what you do physically—it also includes what you look at and what you think about. This is not my opinion, this is what Jesus said, "You have heard that it was said, 'Do not commit adultery.' But I tell you that anyone who looks at a woman lustfully has already committed adultery with her in his heart" (Matthew 5:27–28).

This includes sexual fantasy, pornography, online relationships, and YES, erotica. This seems like a pretty strict standard. Jesus goes on to advise us how to deal with temptation, "If your right eye causes you to sin, gouge it out and throw it away. It is better for you to lose one part of your body than for your whole body to be thrown into hell" (Matthew 5:29 NIV 1984).

His message is clear—get rid of whatever causes you to sin in your heart! Throw out the mommy porn. If it is a portal for temptation, get rid of your iPhone, satellite TV, or your Facebook account. Cut off the relationship that is tempting you. If you really want to know what God says, take His warning seriously. Stop flirting with anything that causes you to think, lust, or fantasize about a man other than your husband.

Is it good for me/us?

This is where things get fuzzy. We don't see anywhere in the Bible where God clearly says no to things like sex toys, masturbation, or oral sex. In fact, you'll find very different opinions from Christian leaders on all these topics. The Corinthian church had questions about "grey" areas, too. Instead of telling them exactly what to do, Paul gave them guidelines on how to use good judgment when the Bible doesn't clearly state something as right or wrong. "'I have the right to do anything,' you say—but not everything is beneficial. 'I have the right to do anything'—but I will not be mastered by anything" (1 Corinthians 6:12).

A few chapters later, Paul seems to repeat himself: "'I have the right to do anything,' you say—but not everything is beneficial. 'I have the right to do anything'—but not everything is constructive. No one should seek their own good, but the good of others" (1 Corinthians 10:23–24).

Here's what you can take from these passages. There are many things in life that you are free to do and enjoy, whether you are single or married. When you are not sure whether something is okay, put it through Paul's filter:

- *Is this beneficial?* Is it good for me? For my husband? Is it good for our marriage?
- *Does it master me?* Can it be habit-forming or addictive?
- *Is it constructive?* Does it help me grow and mature? Does it build our marriage?
- *Is it loving?* Does this action show love toward others or is it selfish?

WHAT ABOUT THOSE GREY AREAS?

Let's run a few of your questions in the grey areas—those not specifically addressed in Scripture—through the grid Juli just set up.

Are erotica and porn okay?

We believe that both porn and erotica are "lustful passions" that awaken an appetite for unrestrained, indiscriminate, sexual desire for men or women other than the person's marriage partner. They both involve mental and visual images of someone you are not married to and often include orgies, glorified fornication/adultery, and homosexuality. And we

65

haven't even gotten to the next question, which brings us to say that entertaining those images is not just between you and your husband or future husband. You're bringing other people into your mind. Finally, it's not beneficial. Throughout this book we've tried to sound the alarm as loudly as we possibly can that you're risking a great deal if you use erotica or porn. Run away as fast as you can!

What's wrong with a married couple watching porn together?

Is this just between the two of you? Not really. By watching them on a screen, you're involving other people. Real people. Push the pause on porn.

Is oral sex okay?

Single girls want to know if oral sex is even sex. Some are thinking it might be a really good outlet for them. The question then becomes: What's the definition of sex? Sex takes place anytime the genitals are intentionally stimulated. It's obvious this takes place during sexual intercourse, right? Well, Ephesians 5:3 says "there must not be even a hint" of sexual sin in your life. Oral sex requires one partner to orally stimulate the genitals of another partner. We think that's more than hinting at sexual sin, don't you?

Married women, we have quite another opinion for you on the matter. Some believe Song of Solomon has two possible steamy scenes poetically describing oral sex between Solomon and his wife (Song of Solomon 2:3 and 4:16). Seems like it's okay within the confines of marriage as long as it is done lovingly and with a desire for the good of the other person.

Is anal sex okay?

We get this question a lot and not everyone agrees. While we don't think it's clearly labeled a sin, we don't think it's beneficial. There is a high risk of infection and illness. We talked to a doctor who simply said, "God made that part of your body an exit, not an entrance." Research the medical risks and pray with your husband before you consider this one.

My husband likes to spank me. Is that okay?

Is it loving? Is it beneficial (physically and emotionally)? If so, *maybe*, but please don't make the mistake of calling it BDSM, which we'll define later. We can only guess that your marriage bed is loving in all ways and at all times, and that there are never bruises, blood, or injury of any kind in any way. Also be sure that you are both equally interested in what we'd prefer to call "sex play." If you have moments of playfulness that include pushing each other around without harm, holding one another up against the wall, or ripping off each other's clothes . . . that's between you and your husband. Be careful not to use rough play as a defense for hurting one another. Frankly, neither of us feels comfortable with this one and we think it gets pretty close to the line of not being beneficial, but we've talked to some very godly women who have a different perspective.

Are sex toys wrong?

Have you ever given your husband a massage with scented oil? Or rubbed his back with a feather? These can be very loving and arousing acts of intimacy and both of them involve "toys." A bottle of lotion is a toy. A feather is a toy. When it comes to toys, we believe you should enjoy a great deal of freedom. We know women who struggled with orgasm for years but were finally able to climax when their husbands used vibrators to stimulate them. We think that's a good thing.

Just be careful with your freedom. With each toy ask, "Is this beneficial? Does it master me? Is it constructive? Is it loving?" If it gets to where you are more interested in a toy than your husband, it might be mastering you. If it leaves a bruise, it's not loving. Use discernment with all things.

Are blindfolding and bondage okay?

Blindfolding cuts off the sense of vision. Anytime you shut off one sense, the others are heightened. If you can lovingly blindfold one another and playfully discover each other's bodies, you may find a heightened sensation. And that's okay, but we'll talk about bondage in the next chapter. It deserves to be dealt with in greater detail.

Is masturbation okay?

This is such a difficult question to answer. Research indicates that most people masturbate at some time in their lives. Yet there is often more shame and guilt surrounding masturbation than there is around adultery.

Opinions vary—even between Juli and me. So we will try to help you form a biblical opinion for yourself.

Whether you are married or not, you can ask yourself this question: "Is this just between the two of us?" Because sex is just for you and your husband or future husband, it would be clear that masturbating while you look at porn or read about a character in a book would be involving another person and would therefore be against God's best plan for your sex life. This would also include making up your own fantasy while you masturbate. It's never beneficial to your marriage or future marriage to focus on a fictional perfect man.

The next question to ask is also useful for both married and single women: "Am I controlled by this?" Masturbation can be very habit-forming. If you can't get through the day without stimulating yourself, it may be compulsive, and that's when it's probably a good idea to seek help.

In fact, if you are struggling with compulsive masturbation or any of these issues, it is important that you ask God to show you who you can tell. You need an older, wiser, godly woman to help you pray and navigate through these things so that you can experience your sexuality inside the boundaries God set when He designed it as a gift for you. So take all your questions to Him in prayer, seeking His wisdom for you and your husband.

AN ANCIENT STRATEGY

People sometimes say that it is "old-fashioned" to define morality based on the Bible, but nothing is more "old-fashioned" than wanting to define right and wrong for ourselves.

Relative morality isn't "progressive"—it's ancient! Let's look back to the beginning of time and see how Satan's strategies haven't changed much.

> The serpent was the shrewdest of all the wild animals the Lord God had made. One day he asked the woman, "Did God really say you must not eat the fruit from any of the trees in the garden?"
>
> "Of course we may eat fruit from the trees in the garden," the woman replied. "It's only the fruit from the tree in the middle of the garden that we are not allowed to eat. God said, 'You must not eat it or even touch it; if you do, you will die.'"
>
> "You won't die!" the serpent replied to the woman. "God knows that your eyes will be opened as soon as you eat it, and you will be like God, knowing both good and evil."
>
> The woman was convinced. She saw that the tree was beautiful and its fruit looked delicious, and she wanted the wisdom it would give her. So she took some of the fruit and ate it. (Genesis 3:1–6 NLT)

Notice that the name of the tree Adam and Eve were not supposed to eat from was "The tree of the knowledge of good and evil" (Genesis 2:17). Think about that name: from the beginning of time, God said it is off-limits for people to define for themselves what is right and what is wrong.

Satan planted doubt in Eve's mind about God's standard, about the consequences of sin, and about God's goodness. He does the same thing today! Can you discern his whisper? Here are two lies he's been whispering to women:

Lie #1: You seriously think there's black and white?

When God clearly states that something is right or wrong, it's not up for debate, discussion, or negotiation. Like it or not, God says some things are wrong, immoral, destructive . . . *sin*. Our society's moral relativism isn't a sign of advancement but is the result of foolishness and pride.

Obviously, erotica confuses standards of right and wrong related to sexual choices. But you don't have to read mommy porn to get those messages—just tune into prime-time television or hang out in the break room at work. Erotica is about pushing the moral envelope even further. One example from the Fifty Shades series is child molestation—something we should clearly recognize as evil. In the story, Christian had a bondage-type sexual relationship with an adult woman for several years when he was a teenager. When he first tells Anastasia about this relationship, she is horrified and calls it abusive. But Christian insists that this woman "was a force for good. What I needed."[16]

Oh, my friend, we are on a slippery slope when we let culture, our intuition, our schools, and our psychologists tell us what is right and wrong. I know it's not politically correct, but are you willing to agree with God that He is the only one who has the right to define morality?

Lie #2: God wants to keep you from pleasure

Satan's greatest assault is to cast doubt on God's motive. He told Eve, "God doesn't really care about you. He wants to keep you in bondage. He knows that if you eat from the tree, you'll be wise like He is. You can't trust Him!"

Satan whispers these lies about sexual standards, too. He paints the "good girl" as the one who misses out on life and the sexually immoral woman as the mature, fulfilled one. Is he right? Is the Christian who follows God's standards really missing out?

Do you really believe that selfishness, fornication, pornography, and sexual perversion are bringing pleasure to people? Is there great joy among those who feel "free" to experiment with bondage, pedophilia, online sex, and homosexuality? Do we realize that every choice to compromise sexually is more than a moral failure? It is a choice away from the ultimate joy and pleasure for which we were created.

God is the greatest proponent of your pleasure. Do you believe that? Not the pleasure that is sweet for a season but the deep, profound satisfaction that only grows sweeter with time.

Pull Back the Shades

Who defines right and wrong in your choices? Do you believe God's standards are for your good? Take a question you've been wrestling with regarding sexuality and put it through the filter of His Word. What did you find? Write about it.

Chapter 5

Since When Does Prince Charming Carry Handcuffs?

Once upon a time, there was a beautiful, young woman who was also very lonely. She desperately wanted a handsome, brave man to recognize her beauty and fall madly in love with her. Then he would carry her off to his "Red Room of Pain," ask her to sign a contract giving him permission to punish, possess, and control her. But it was all very romantic because she consented to being sexually tortured and, in some odd way, found it stimulating.

Is there any question that the paragraph above is twisted and evil? Apparently, there is, or millions of Christian women would not be reading *Fifty Shades of Grey*. Because of the series, BDSM (bondage, dominance, sadism, and masochism)—once clearly stigmatized as dark and uncommon—is being normalized and applauded . . . and coming to a bedroom near you. It's such a growing phenomenon that you have to be armed with an understanding of it to be able to talk with friends—or maybe to figure it out for yourself. We need to note that Susan Quilliam, a British relationship psychologist and sex advice columnist, was quoted in an ABC News report, saying, *"Fifty Shades* has been roundly criticized by the BDSM community and its depiction of the lifestyle is inaccurate. Christian Grey's initial seduction of Anastasia breaks every rule in the BDSM book." She goes on to say "the relationship portrayed in the book is exploitive on both sides and therefore emotionally unsafe and not sane."[17]

American journalist Lisa Ling decided to enter into the world of BDSM to see what it is really like. Her show, which aired on the Oprah Winfrey Network, featured men hiring women they didn't even know to strip them to their underwear, blindfold, and beat them. One married couple who likes it rough went to a BDSM bed-and-breakfast where they could choose to have others "play" with them. I could not get my spirit to reconcile the visual images of her program with the shockingly pleasant, approving tone of Ling's voice as she commentated.

As I expressed my concern with a Christian friend, she was shocked to find out that I didn't approve of BDSM. We debated it in front of a few friends and then she pulled me aside to privately tell me that she and her husband like "spanking." That brings up an important, though obvious, question:

WHAT EXACTLY IS BDSM?

BDSM is an acronym for Bondage, Dominance, Sadism, and Masochism. In psychiatry, the terms *sadism* and *masochism* describe a personality type characterized by a person deriving pleasure and gratification from inflicting physical pain and humiliation. The terms specifically refer to one who either enjoys giving pain (sadist) or one who enjoys receiving pain (masochist).

Bondage is tying, binding, or restraining someone for sexual or psychological pleasure and is one tool of the sadist. Rope, cuffs, tape, or other restraints are used. *Dominance* is the role of a sadist who is taking authority over the "submissive" in various ways including domestic servitude, verbal humiliation, sexual slavery, fetishes (such as shoe/boot worship), erotic humiliation, whipping, making the submissive a human toilet, or forcing the submissive to have sex with another partner while watching.[18]

Why so graphic? Because we want you to be very clear what you or others are referring to when using the acronym. The fact is we shouldn't let the world abbreviate these words. Whenever you shorten it to BDSM, be sure to connect it to the true meaning. It's a lot easier to "defend" the letters BDSM than it is to extol the virtues of bondage, dominance, sadism, and masochism.

We want to be very clear about something we've already told you: sex play is not the same as BDSM. Sexual play, even within marriage, crosses the line if it ever causes physical harm, is degrading, or violates your will.

❖   ❖   ❖

If you haven't read the series, Christian introduces Ana to his BDSM world in the beginning of their relationship. He refuses to touch her sexually until she reviews the "rules," sees his "playroom" (aka the Red Room of Pain), and signs a contract, spelling out an agreement of their bondage. Here is some of the wording in the contract:

> The Submissive accepts the Dominant as her master, with the understanding that she is now the property of the Dominant, to be dealt with as the Dominant pleases . . . The Submissive shall accept whippings, floggings, spankings, canings, paddlings, or any other discipline the Dominant should decide to administer, without hesitation, inquiry, or complaint.[19]

Ana never signs the contract but asks Christian for some mixture of a romantic relationship with elements of the bondage, punishment, and the sexual "playroom." Eventually, these BDSM elements become part of their marriage bed and all seem to flow nicely with a loving though quite controlling relationship.

Although *Fifty Shades* is fiction, we assure you that the world of BDSM is not. Since the book's release there has been a dramatic increase in the sales of bondage gear.[20] What was once viewed as a strange, aberrant practice is becoming increasingly mainstream for married couples and for those looking for an exciting affair.

WHAT'S THE DRAW?

You might be wondering, "Why on earth would any reasonable woman want to be caned, whipped, or chained by her lover? Who would ever want to call a man 'Master' and be treated like property?" We believe it ultimately stems back to the deep longings we introduced in chapter 1 and we want to discuss this in a bit more detail now. But our longings are complicated and the answers to those questions aren't as simple as you might think.

"I want to be sexually alive."

First of all, people want to be sexually alive and this requires sexual excitement. They are bored with "vanilla" sex. When you try something new and a little dangerous, chemicals, like adrenaline and norepinephrine, course through your body. Add to that mix natural painkillers like dopamine and endorphins that are released when your body is harmed. This combination along with sexual arousal is *powerful* and can create an incredible sexual experience. For those who view seeking physical pleasure as the *only* reason for sex, they may be willing to try anything to achieve the next sexual high. If this describes you, we will show you in chapter 7 how to build an exciting sex life within godly principles of mutual love and respect.

"I want to be emotionally whole."

Others are drawn into BDSM relationships for emotional reasons. BDSM plays upon the most intense of all human experiences: fear, sexual arousal, shame, control, and authority. Many have endured emotional, physical, or sexual trauma in childhood in which these themes were all mixed together. Instead of being loving, authority was used to harm or humiliate. Maybe sex was employed as a weapon to control and was laden with both physical pleasure and intense fear.

When I've worked with children who were physically or sexually abused, I often used dolls or a big sand tray as a tool. Kids can't always say what happened or how it affected them, but they can act it out. So they would use little figurines or dolls to "play out" what happened to them and how it affected them.

The same is true with adults who have been traumatized. Without knowing it, they may re-create past abusive dynamics in their present relationships. Maybe they are drawn to those who overpower or victimize them. In other situations, they become the person in control—the person perhaps abusing a child or weak adult.

The draw to relive trauma is very powerful. Like a magnet, you can feel compelled to master it or find a way to make it end differently. BDSM may seem to be the perfect solution. Instead of "playing" like a kid with dolls to re-create the trauma, you can "play" in real life. In fact, some people claim that BDSM can be therapeutic. The Fifty Shades series tiptoes right up to this conclusion.

When Anastasia meets with Christian's therapist, Dr. Flynn, she asks about Christian's infatuation with sadism, knowing full well that her boyfriend was abused as a child. The doctor rolls his eyes dramatically. "That's no longer recognized as a psychiatric term . . . This is a pet peeve of mine . . . Of course, there's such a thing as sexual sadism, but it's not a disease; it's a lifestyle choice. And if it's practiced in a safe, sane relationship between consenting adults, then it's a non-issue."[21]

"Dr. Flynn" is correct that the brilliant minds of psychiatry have decided that gaining sexual pleasure from hurting someone or being hurt is perfectly fine as long as it is consensual. We have seen a dramatic shift in how the psychological community approaches many sexual practices, including cross-dressing, homosexuality, and even sexual attraction to children. We need to be very careful who we allow to define our view of healthy sex.

I strongly disagree with those (like the fictional Dr. Flynn) who claim BDSM is helpful or even neutral. In fact, I think it is playing with fire.

BDSM presents shadows of a much darker world—a world of true bondage. As I read Fifty Shades, I was struck by how much the "bondage" language mirrored spiritual things. Obeying a person completely and calling them "Master" are attitudes and actions we should reserve for Jesus. For a while, I had trouble listening to one of my favorite Christy Nockels worship songs, "My Master," because of how that word was exploited in these books. There really is a very dark, powerful world of bondage that goes beyond ropes and handcuffs. I have a dear friend who was once enslaved in BDSM against her will. When I told her about this chapter I was writing, she wrote this to share with you:

I grew up in a family whose parents embraced a BDSM lifestyle. I also experienced it personally in the trenches of child sex trafficking, molestation, and satanic worship. Although it was all I knew, it changed me—the way I viewed myself, the way I saw marriage, the way I understood sexual intimacy, and ultimately the way I viewed God.

I try to forget the bondage, the dominance, and the sadomasochism branded into my being and into my heart, but I can't. The scars on my flesh and in my mind remain. For no matter how hard I try to run from the memories, they are still vividly present: The handcuffs on my wrists dig into my flesh and the chains on my neck rattle as my pimp (the person who I called "the master") chokes me, reminding me of the contract I signed so many years ago. I shiver. Time stands still.

Now that I have been removed from these situations and have been learning about the heart of Jesus, I don't understand how some people can see BDSM as play and games. I believe strongly that the nucleus of BDSM is satanism. It is an arena for him to gain ground in the lives of many people. How can BDSM be an optional part of a normal life or a healthy relationship—where a person embraces one aspect of bondage and not another? It is a doorway that leads a person into much heartache, pain, grief, and despair, leading to a lifestyle of destruction— the definition of my story.

My friend's chilling words remind us that we are either in bondage or we are free. How can we who have been redeemed by God "play" with the enemy's tools of enslavement?

Read the words of Isaiah spoken by Jesus, our Redeemer, "The Spirit of the Lord is upon me, for he has anointed me to bring Good News to the poor. He has sent me to proclaim that captives will be released, that the blind will see, that the oppressed will be set free" (Luke 4:18 NLT).

It was for our freedom that Jesus died! Our entire being—including our sexuality—should be an expression of God's redeeming love.

"I want a strong man."

Finally, the BDSM theme in erotica can also be attractive for a woman who wants a take-charge man. They are longing to be protected by a strong man but can't find one. Instead, they settle for anything that seems to resemble strength. Research indicates that women involved in BDSM are more likely to act as the submissive than the dominant. One survey found that 89 percent of females active in the BDSM lifestyle preferred playing the submissive. Conversely, 71 percent of men preferred dominating.[22]

This supports a growing trend we have observed. We hear from women all the time who desperately want their husbands to be decisive leaders and single women who wonder why guys won't take the initiative to make a commitment. The passivity of men is also finding its way into the bedroom. I've noticed a dramatic increase in the number of husbands who won't initiate sexually or who seem to have little appetite for sex with their wives.

BDSM can appeal to women who are desperate to have a man act more like a man. We believe this longing is rooted in the intentional creation of God. As resourceful as you may be, you were created with the desire to lean upon a strong man. The relationship between husband and wife was designed to mirror Christ's relationship to His bride, the church. Ephesians 5 clearly says that the man models Christ's leadership and the woman models the church's submission. Because our culture has rejected the notion of female submission and male leadership, the deep hunger to return to how we were created to function leads us to counterfeits—like BDSM.

Is it possible that women are finding an outlet for their hunger for a strong man by reading about a distortion of one? While many of them may never actually try BDSM, reading about it is a cheap validation of what their hearts are starved to experience.

Solving the "weak man" problem with BDSM is about as logical as curing obesity by promoting anorexia. Both are dangerous distortions of appetite. The true answer is for us to grasp what health looks like. Christ taught and modeled that authoritative leadership is for the purpose of loving sacrifice, not domination, control, abuse, or humiliation.

SINCE WHEN DOES PRINCE CHARMING CARRY HANDCUFFS?

SO, WHAT IS HEALTHY POWER?

When I got married nineteen years ago, some of my friends were aghast that I used the "s" word in my wedding vows (I'm referring to the nine-letter one: *submission*). Why, all of a sudden, is it now sexy to call a man "master"? Because there is something wonderfully romantic about God's original design of a "prince charming" who knows how to lovingly lead. I can say without any doubt that my decision to honor my husband as the leader in our marriage has been a powerful ingredient in the deep love, including the sexual love, we now share with each other.

Submission is all about power—not weakness. Many believe that God tells women to submit in marriage because He wants them to be weak. The exact opposite is really true. Women have incredible power in marriage: the power to destroy their husbands or the power to build them up. Proverbs 14:1 says, "The wise woman builds her house, but with her own hands the foolish one tears hers down." Our culture has embraced the foolishness of using the power of women to destroy the strength and valor of men. God's design for a wife to submit is not to take away her power but to channel it in a way that builds a courageous lover and leader in her husband. God's plan works! (If you want to know how this plays out practically in marriage, you can read more about this in my book *Finding the Hero in Your Husband*.)

❖   ❖   ❖

If the idea of biblical submission causes your feathers to ruffle, I understand. I, unlike Juli, did not use the "s" word in my wedding vows. In the early years of my marriage, when Bob and I were sorting out all of our brokenness, I was starved for a strong man, but I was using my power to "tear my house down." Oh, I was the good Christian woman who submitted to my husband with a martyr's heart if he asked me to move across the nation and start a new life. But God forgive him if he should suggest where we park at church on Sunday morning! Our actions betray our beliefs. Though not a proverbial card-carrying feminist, my actions proved that I was a strong believer in the strength and superiority of my womanhood and I used it to crush my husband's strength with every small decision. In this way, my heart was at war with God.

You cannot stay in a position of opposition to God and His intended design for your life without eventually thirsting for what you were created to experience. And you were created to experience a mutual, loving relationship in which the man in your life is given the freedom to lead and be strong.

I was in a hotel in Australia when the thirst became too much for me. It was after a long day of sightseeing during which I'd emasculated my dear husband with every decision. The tipping point was when he suggested we take our car back to the hotel before we met my parents. I demanded we park it where we were and meet them straightaway. For the first time, I realized how ugly I was when I saw his heart through his eyes. It was crushed. "Dear God," I prayed. "What have I done?" I cried and pleaded with God for forgiveness until about 2:00 in the morning. I realized that my feminist independence had only resulted in isolation and loneliness. As if my heart had been cleansed by the tears, I felt prompted to awaken my husband and do something so submissive that it could only have come from the heart of God. I began by apologizing for the way I'd used my strength to crush his. I even told him that I had no idea how I would ever change my habits but that I would try. I kneeled before him as I spoke these words so that I could symbolically express my honor of him. I had a bowl of warm water at his feet. Lovingly, I washed them, soothing both his body and his heart. This was my surrender—to Bob, yes, but even more to God's plan for affirming and supporting him. My once-feminist hands finally became truly, powerfully feminine! We both cried beautiful tears of intimacy.

The very next day Bob began to do things for me that made me feel cherished. He held the door for me, put his hand on the small of my back to protectively lead me, and I don't believe I've carried a piece of luggage since that day. He is a strong man who leads our family well. Something rose up in him when I honored his strength. We truly do have the power to build up or tear down men. I have done both, and building them up is far more fruitful.

I must admit, old habits die hard. I did not instantly become—in fact, I'm still often not—a submissive woman. But I have learned the beauty of true submission. And my heart is not so eager to wander toward counterfeits.

Satan is forever dangling counterfeits of God's beauty before our eyes. Erotica and BDSM are simply his latest tricks to lasso the hearts of women. Please don't take the bait! If you thirst for a strong man or emotional healing, can I kindly ask if you are seeking the real thing or if you are feeding your craving with a twisted counterfeit?

Pull Back the Shades

Is your longing for a strong man being met in a biblical manner or with counterfeits that blur the lines of abuse? Does your heart resist or embrace the kindness of submission? Write it out, because this one can be hard to wrap your head around. Make an intentional choice to follow God's best plan for your life!

Chapter 6

Don't Let the Red Room
Destroy Your Bedroom

Whether you're married or single, perhaps the most obvious reason you might consider reading erotica is to awaken or satisfy sexual desire. Dr. Oz featured an entire series of shows on *Fifty Shades of Grey*, claiming that the book might be the cure for the female libido. He asked two couples who were having problems with their sex life to read the book. They described their sex life before the book as infrequent and mundane. After they'd read it? Well, one couple who previously was hard-pressed to have sex more than six times a year reported having sex twice a week now. The other: twice a night.

On the program, Dr. Laura Berman, a well-known sex therapist, had this simple suggestion for millions of women who want great sex lives: "Read erotica." A lot of experts out there say it'll be good for your sex life and great for your marriage.

Are their claims true?

While God's opinion is our first consideration, we also keep coming back to the *long-term* outcome of women who've used erotica to meet the longings of their hearts, and we do not see a long-term satisfaction.

Trisha found out the hard way that erotica simply wasn't

enough and that forced her into a progression to seek heightened pleasure elsewhere. She sent us a picture of her beautiful family. Three children and an adoring husband surround her—each with matching shirts and matching smiles. They are a clean-cut, all-American, Christian family that almost didn't make it. Here is what Trisha wrote:

> I am a Christ-following woman. I was introduced to erotica and porn at a young age. When my husband and I were dating, we viewed porn . . . it was fun and I loved fantasy, so this went right along with the thoughts in my head. Before long, the fantasies haunted me. I couldn't get them out of my head. This not only held true during sexual intimacy with my husband but just in normal, everyday life. I was constantly thinking about it.

To escalate the intensity of what she once enjoyed but was no longer satisfying her, she began to look for new ways to get the high she needed.

> While "researching" masturbation, I came across women's stories. Stories about masturbation and being with female lovers. An introduction to something new! Though I felt horribly guilty and knew I was wrong, it had a horrible hold on me.

What once was a tool she'd hoped would bring her and her husband together for great sex became something that drew her away from him. Sex with him just wasn't that thrilling anymore—and the idea of having sex with a woman became more and more appealing. Nothing seemed able to satisfy her.

While erotica might originally heighten sexual feelings, over the long haul it erodes something much more important—intimacy. Whether you are married or single, you are looking for more than sex. Your body, your mind, and your spirit were created to crave intimacy. Earlier we introduced the word used in the Old Testament for sex: *yada*—to know, to be known, to be deeply respected. Transcending the physical act, God's language speaks of the deep emotional knowing you ultimately long to experience. The physical aspect of sex is just one part of the equation, but our culture tends to hyperfocus on it with no attention to the ultimately more fulfilling aspect of *yada*—emotional intimacy. Sexual activity by itself is an empty substitute for true intimacy, and will never be enough.

Erotica places undue emphasis on the physical and disables your ability to connect emotionally. No matter how much you may want to believe that the Red Room of Pain will bring the high you are seeking, it's much more likely to destroy your bedroom. To set the record straight, here's an expert I trust much more than Dr. Oz or Dr. Laura Berman, my friend and yours—Dr. Juli!

◆   ◆   ◆

PORN AND EROTICA MAKE SEX
EMOTIONALLY UNSAFE

In marriage, you can build sexual excitement in one of two ways: by looking more closely into each other (true intimacy) or creating a fantasy outside of each other (counterfeit intimacy). Couples who really "get it" know how to fully share their sexuality—how to communicate the most intimate of experiences with and without words. Being emotionally naked like this makes you extremely vulnerable. Both you and your husband have to feel completely safe to let go, to share thoughts, desires, and physical sensations. The journey toward marital intimacy is learning to create the safest environment possible so that you can explore together without fear of betrayal or humiliation. Erotica and porn do the exact opposite. They will make your bedroom an emotional land mine.

Let me put it this way: I don't know any woman who is genuinely happy to make love to her husband while he is thinking about another naked woman. How humiliating and degrading to be giving your body to a man who is sexually aroused only because he is imagining another woman!

What do you think happens when people watch porn or read erotica? They are storing in their minds private, erotic images that can be recalled during sex. The normal lumpy bodies, the bland bedroom, the mundane movements can be imagined away and replaced by whatever scene or image will create a sexual high. This is offensive to wives and husbands alike. Here's what one man shared with us about erotica:

Can I throw my hat in the ring as a husband and say that I would be utterly humiliated if I discovered my wife was viewing or reading anything in place of or connected to my loving offering!! It would be a HUGE kick in the drawers that would be very effective at removing my masculinity!

Eventually, a couple who has fallen into this trap learns to lie to each other or they simply have sex without ever sharing feelings, thoughts, and their experience. Their bodies may be intertwined but their minds and hearts couldn't be further apart. "What are you thinking about?" becomes a very dangerous question during sex.

EROTICA SHIFTS THE FOCUS FROM US TO ME

The average man and woman are so different physiologically and emotionally that they can never enjoy the greatest sexual pleasure together until they learn to communicate, to listen, and to delay their own pleasure in order to please the other. By God's design, selfish sex will always miss the mark.

Porn and erotica are selfish sex, requiring no sacrifice and no effort to love another person. You can have what you want, when you want, and how you want it. The problem is, it's all fake. The more you chase the counterfeit, the further away you get from the real deal—intimacy. Becoming a great lover requires you to exercise the muscles of temporarily suspending what you want in order to understand and bring joy to your husband. Instead, erotica teaches you to selfishly chase after your immediate desire with no thought of love.

How wonderful—but so very challenging—that God made it absolutely impossible for two people to be sexually satisfied long-term without sacrificing for one another. For a few months, a couple can be lost in their own little quest for sexual pleasure and find some fulfillment. But ultimately, both a man and woman will find this to be an empty pursuit.

ENOUGH WILL NEVER BE ENOUGH

There are a lot of brain chemicals involved in sex. What you look at and what you think about has a powerful impact on what chemicals are flowing at any given time. When a couple in a committed relationship has sex, their bodies release endorphins and oxytocin. These two chemicals lead to feelings of closeness and bonding and also a general sense of well-being. They help reduce stress, promote sound sleep, pain relief, and even may help slow the aging process. Frequent intercourse in marriage literally helps a husband and wife feel closely connected as they weather the storms of life together.

When a person has a new, exciting sexual experience, the body releases different chemicals, including phenylethylamine (PEA) and adrenaline. The combination of these two is powerful—much stronger than the steady impact of oxytocin and endorphins. In fact, PEA and adrenaline impact the brain in a way similar to crack cocaine.[23] A person becomes intoxicated with sexual pleasure. God designed this as a wonderful treasure for young lovers to experience on their honeymoon as they venture into sexuality together.

The problem is that PEA and adrenaline will only reappear as sexual experiences continue to be new, exciting, and sometimes even dangerous. What created the sexual "high" last month is no longer new. Like Trisha, a woman (or couple) must constantly push the envelope to find a fantasy, image, or experience that brings back the sexual high. This is exactly what we see happening as women read erotica. From Kelly:

> I progressed from seemingly harmless romantic stories to online erotica and eventually to porn. The erotica sites have links to porn sites. I never thought I would click on them in the beginning. I was even disgusted by the images at first. However, I became increasingly numb as time went on and I soon found myself on those very porn sites I thought I would never, ever visit.

For some, reading erotica eventually leads to acting out sexually when words on a page no longer meet the need. *The Huffington Post* reported an increase in extramarital sex as a result of the increase in the use of erotica. AshleyMadison. com, an extramarital affair dating site, discovered a 50 percent boost in members confessing to indulging in bondage role-play with lovers—*not husbands and wives*—after reading *Fifty Shades of Grey*. They claim 62 percent of all new members signed up because they were interested in trying BDSM and feared their spouse would be shocked if they suggested it.[24]

Not all women who read erotica end up in addictions or affairs. Some just don't need a real person to be physically fulfilled anymore. They progress in their own private self-pleasuring and mental imagery. Many of the single women we spoke to reported they no longer want to go through the hard work of dating or getting to know a guy once they taste erotica. Married women often said they became more and more unsatisfied with their husbands. *SELF* magazine and *The New Yorker* ran articles on this phenomenon in recent years. They both suggested that if you want to have a great sex life either now or in the future, you better say no to porn!

GREAT ICING WON'T SAVE A BAD CAKE

Some couples flock to porn to turn up the heat in their bedroom because they believe great sex can somehow compensate for their lack of intimacy in other areas. Sex is a wonderful gift when it is embraced as the "icing on the cake." Have you ever baked a fallen cake? Opened the oven to find a huge pit in the center of your creation? Once when this happened to me, I tried to cover up the crater with icing. To my chagrin, the icing took the form of the cake.

The same is true with sex in marriage. It will always take on the form of the relationship, even for couples that try to use it to cover up other problems or to think of it as a separate issue. Many couples come to counseling complaining of problems sexually. Almost invariably, their sexual dynamics are a perfect illustration of what is happening throughout their entire relationship.

One young wife I recently met with was devastated that her husband had little interest is sex. She explained, "When we were dating, he couldn't keep his hands off me. All he talked about was how much fun we would have sexually. Now that we've been married for a year, he doesn't seem to want me. I feel completely unattractive and humiliated."

As we explored the emotional dynamics of this couple, it became evident that the wife was a very strong woman married to a laid-back young man. Their passionate romance had quickly turned into more of a "mother-son" relationship in which she chided and criticized her husband. His emotional retreat from showing strength and leadership made its way to the bedroom. He fell into the habit of using pornography and masturbation to meet his sexual needs rather than risk being "less than a man" with his wife.

I doubt that the best "sex therapy" alone could revive this couple's sex life. First, they had to work on the quality and nature of their intimacy. They both were making choices in daily life that created an emotional land mine in their bedroom.

I believe strongly that a great sex life in marriage can build upon and strengthen emotional and spiritual intimacy. However, sexual intimacy even within marriage will be an empty substitute for love.

WHAT'S MORE IMPORTANT THAN ORGASM?

If God created and defines sex as a "deep knowing," we can reason that the ultimate sexual satisfaction will be found when we are truly known by one another. An *American Health Journal* study of over two thousand married women discovered two startling findings concerning sexual satisfaction. First, although much has been made of the female orgasm, findings indicated that there was little correlation between a woman's ability to orgasm and reporting a high level of sexual satisfaction. Second, there was a very strong correlation between sexual satisfaction and meaningful friendship between spouses.[25] Translation: If you want a satisfying sex life—to truly experience *yada*—friendship with your husband is the pathway to achieve it.

I know a little something about this. The first year of our marriage was horrible! On one level, Bob and I were deeply committed and in love with each other. On another level, we just couldn't find one another's hearts. Sex was of paramount importance to me during this season of distance because I believed it would solve all our problems. I was chasing the big O but the physical act of sex wasn't going to fix what ailed us. Our problems were bigger than we realized. Both of us had carried different types of sexual sin into our marriage that we both hoped would fade away after our wedding.

I had a mind filled with memories of sinful sexual acts I had committed before marriage. The pictures were often there in my head when Bob and I would fight. (I'll address that more thoroughly later in the book. It's a big deal!) But how could I tell my sweet husband that I was struggling with this? He didn't even know that I was not a virgin on our wedding night!

A sweet counselor named Tippy began to unravel the lies in my heart about sex and relationship. She helped both Bob and me go through the hard work of laying our ugly hearts bare before one another.

It was not easy.

In differing stages of confession, repentance, waiting, and prayer, we began to grow in emotional intimacy. At the end of it, we both knew *all* of the other person, we loved each other more, and truly experienced *yada*. There's something really freeing about having Bob know all my secrets . . . and still choosing to love me. In that context, my heart and my body are both free to be naked before him and engulfed in his tenderness and touch. Though my heart was fully healed after many years of hard work, my body still needed a little bit of work.

We decided to work with a Christian sex therapist, and even then our work was so much about our hearts. Her homework was always prefaced with: "Before you do this homework assignment, spend two hours in platonic friendship together." It seemed so nonlinear to my type-A personality. We might have a fifteen-minute homework assignment, but our therapist wanted us to spend two hours lying in the grass looking at the fireflies! Good grief!

Well, all I can say is this: now Bob and I really like fireflies. They remind us to be *very* good friends (wink!). The problem was not our bodies but our hearts. We needed to grow in intimate friendship. To be known.

When the deep knowing is given priority in our love lives, the physical aspect of sex just works better. For example, one of the most statistically accurate studies on sexuality ever conducted in the United States determined that the most orgasmic women are middle-aged, married, conservative Protestant women with 32 percent claiming that they climax every time they have sex.[26] I like to call that the revenge of the church ladies! (For the record, I have a great sex life but it's not *that* great. So don't sweat it if yours isn't either.) In reality, this speaks less about sexual satisfaction and more about emotional satisfaction. You see, the not-so-obvious fact is this: these women were already full. They were intimately connected to God, and I believe that opens the door for them to be more emotionally connected to their spouse. In this context, the physical aspect of sex is a bonus to the deep knowing. If you are looking for satisfaction for your longings, you need much more than sexual revival. You need a spiritual one, too.

In the next two chapters, we'll help you move toward both sexual *and* spiritual revival!

Pull Back the Shades

How you been pursuing false intimacy?
What is one step you can take to pursue
true intimacy with your husband or
with friends? (You can find some great
suggestions in appendix 2, What Do I Do
with My Struggle?)

Chapter 7

The Sexually Satisfied Woman

One of the biggest issues I help newly married women walk through is sexual repression that was rooted in their years of singleness. The church has *majored* on playing *defense* on the topic of sex. In an effort to keep teens chaste, women modest, and men monogamous, the primary message coming out of the church is DON'T: don't look, don't touch, don't think or feel sexually. This has resulted in Christian women who are confused about whether sexual pleasure is really okay. The two most common causes of their sexual barriers are ironically polar opposites. Some Christian women were so hyper-focused on sexual purity as singles that, as married women, now they're struggling to find the freedom to be sexual. Other Christian women carry the guilt and scars of sexual sin and need healing. As you know, I fell into the second camp.

I was well into my journey of sexual healing and wholeness when I discovered there were still remnants of frigidity lurking deep down inside of me. Oh, I thought I'd found my ability to be free, but one night, as Bob and I were planning to meet for a sexual rendezvous, I realized there were still barriers in my brain!

In the middle of high school kids' sports schedules and

overwhelming careers, I sent Bob a romantic text with a time-sensitive twist. "Honey, romantic dinner at 6:00. Don't arrive one moment before 6:00 . . . or one moment after 6:00. And we only have until 7:00."

At 3:00, I threw a frozen ham loaf in the oven and went back to my computer to finish up my work. At 5:45, I sautéed some green beans and mashed up some red potatoes, smothered them both in butter, and plopped them on either side of the ham loaf.

I'd been reading *The Love Dare* and I believe it told me to dress a little sexy. Me? Sexy? I'm the modesty queen. I write books about modesty and speak about it all over the country. I don't have anything sexy to wear. Cute? Yes. Fashionable? Oh yes! Sexy? No. I ran upstairs and threw on a blouse that I normally wear with a tank top underneath. It looked to be a little lower cut, so that'd do. When I came down to check on the green beans, I realized that my black blouse was also see-through. Entirely! (That must be why I wear it with a tank.) My immediate thought was, *I can't wear this!* But as I began to run upstairs with the clock ticking away, I thought, *I* can *wear this!* And I did. Dannah Gresh, the modesty queen, wore a sexy shirt for her husband! If it were Rihanna at the Grammys sporting her lacy black bra for the paparazzi, it'd be completely inappropriate. But it was Dannah in the kitchen with her husband, and he loved it. I marveled at how his eyes kept shifting from that ham loaf to . . . well, you know! I absolutely loved how I mesmerized him.

But as I looked back over the evening, I knew how difficult

it had been for me to enjoy the sexual freedom God has given to me as a Christian woman. This may be true of you, also, so Juli and I are going to give you a pep talk!

THE RECIPE FOR SEXUAL PLEASURE

There seems to be a great dividing wall between the spiritual side of a woman and her sexuality. While Bible studies can help her with anxiety, her friendships, and even her marriage, how could something Christian possibly be of help in the bedroom?

We've got news for you: God is not about just playing defense on the topic of sex. His message doesn't just include a big, fat NO. He created sex and He is all for it! In fact, God is for great, pleasurable, and frequent sex within the context of marriage.

Whether you are married or single, it is very important for you to get this: the world does not hold the recipe for sexual pleasure. If you want a great sex life now or in the future, put down *Cosmo* and pick up the Bible. I know that sounds hard to believe, but I think we can prove it to you. The Bible has some pretty specific and steamy things to say about great sex.

GOD GIVES WOMEN PERMISSION TO ACKNOWLEDGE SEXUAL NEEDS

Growing up, I was one of those "good Christian girls" who took the message of purity seriously. I had trained my mind and my heart to say no to sexual things through my teens and early twenties. When I got married, the wedding ring on my finger didn't suddenly erase all the "no" messages. I had a very difficult time accepting that now it was a good thing for me to pursue and enjoy sex. In fact, for the first decade of my marriage, I wrongly believed men were supposed to enjoy sex and a loving, unselfish wife was to do her "wifely duty."

Then, I actually looked at the "wifely duty" verse. Here it is:

> The husband should fulfill his marital duty to his wife, and likewise the wife to her husband. The wife does not have authority over her own body but yields it to her husband. In the same way, the husband does not have authority over his own body but yields it to his wife. Do not deprive each other except by mutual consent and for a time, so that you may devote yourselves to prayer. Then come together again so that Satan will not tempt you because of your lack of self-control. (1 Corinthians 7:3–5)

Notice that before Paul even addresses the husband's sexual needs, he mentions the wife's needs. Do you see it? It says that women have sexual needs that their husbands are required to meet—a "husbandly duty."

I've talked to many Christian women who are ashamed to even admit that they have sexual needs that may or may not be met in marriage. God knows you are a sexual being. He made you that way. Therefore, according to Paul, one of the primary reasons men and women should seek marriage is because of these sexual desires and needs.

GOD GIVES COUPLES PERMISSION
TO BE SEXUALLY ADVENTUROUS

You've heard of the term "missionary position," right? But did you know that European missionaries actually taught that this was the most acceptable way for a couple to make love? It's a funny term that hints toward a subtle lie that many Christian women believe, "It's okay to enjoy sex a little bit, but let's not get carried away. New positions, new adventures, new pleasures—that's all just a little too worldly!"

If you're married, the Bible has quite a different message for you: *Do* get carried away—far away! Be adventurous, be playful, be passionate, go crazy with your husband. You don't need the Fifty Shades trilogy to give you ideas. Can I suggest a biblical source of passionate encouragement? Song of Solomon.

The first several times I read this little book of the Bible, I'll admit I didn't quite get it. I'm not a poetic soul, so I didn't appreciate all the flowery talk about fruits, animals, and plants. Then my friend Linda Dillow encouraged me to read it again, but with different eyes. "Notice everything Solomon's bride did as a lover. What can you learn about being a lover to your husband?"

The first thing I noticed was that this woman wasn't waiting around for her husband—she went after passion. She dreamed about her husband, thought about his naked body, and planned for sexual adventures. She creatively used everything at her disposal—her words, her body, fragrances, and foods—to celebrate their sexuality. I affectionately began to call this woman "The Smokin' Hot Mama."

If you are married, it is right and godly and holy to pursue great pleasure in sexual intimacy with your husband. I feel so strongly about this message that Linda and I published a Bible study on this topic called *Passion Pursuit: What Kind of Love Are You Making?* It's time for Christians to start playing offense—to reclaim the gift of sexual pleasure as it was created to be experienced.

YOUR PATHWAY TO PLEASURE

God has designed every woman with her own unique pathway to sexual pleasure. Imagine that you are cleaning up the dishes after dinner and your husband gets that gleam in his eye. He wants you. How do you switch gears from being a housewife, mom, or accountant all the way to being a Smokin' Hot Mama lover? By learning to walk down your pathway.

God's design is for you to understand your own and your husband's pathway to sexual pleasure. Your pathway to pleasure has road signs along it. Some of them say, "This feels great!" "I love being so close to my husband," or "Oh, I really want this." But there are also obstacles and stop signs on the way to arousal. Thoughts like "I just can't get into this," "I'd feel stupid if I just let go," "I'm so self-conscious about the roll of fat around my stomach," or, "I wonder if he's really thinking about me?"

When you run into these obstacles, you may shut down sexually or you might choose a "shortcut," like erotica. Instead of working through the barrier, you recall an image or erotic memory to propel you to sexual response. The more often you "shortcut," the less skilled you become in following your authentic pathway to sexual intimacy.

Instead, be willing to do the work to remove the boulders on your path and to tear down the stop signs. Every married couple will run into a brick wall somewhere in their sexual journey together. After a halfhearted effort to break through the problem, many couples give up. They settle for a less-than-satisfying sex life, they endure mediocre intimacy, or they channel their sexual desire into fantasies fueled by outside sources.

My message to you is, "Don't give up the fight." The greatest lovers are those who have learned to tenaciously address roadblocks along the pathway together. Whether it's a porn addiction, pain during intercourse, inability to have an orgasm, terrible memories from sexual abuse, a past betrayal, or a total disconnect in sexual desire, many couples before you have found victory together through the grace and wisdom of Christ Jesus.

We know more about sexual function, physiology, and the impact of trauma than ever before. Find a Christian expert and/or mentor who can help you through the barriers that you and your husband may be facing. If you're not ready for that step, we recommend *The Gift of Sexual Fulfillment* or *Restoring the Pleasure*, which are both written by Clifford and Joyce Penner. These books will definitely help clear the pathway of obstacles.

USE YOUR BRAIN TO GIVE YOU THE GREEN LIGHT

Consider this: erotic literature is nothing but words on a page. No pictures, no sound, no touch, yet it is able to create intense sexual desire and arousal in most women. Why? Because the mind is a powerful sex organ. The brain controls whether there is a "no trespassing" sign or a glaring "GO!" sign on your pathway. The right words, the right images, and the right use of imagination can get your sexual motor into gear.

The Smokin' Hot Mama was smokin' hot because she thought about her husband sexually. In fact, she fantasized about him. Here is an example:

> My lover is dark and dazzling,
> better than ten thousand others! . . .
> His arms are like rounded bars of gold,
> set with beryl.
> His body is like bright ivory,
> glowing with lapis lazuli. (Song of Solomon 5:10,
> 14 NLT)

The authors of *Intimate Allies* make this statement about the nature of the Smokin' Hot Mama's thinking: "After commenting on his strong arms, she then describes a part of his body as polished ivory. Most English translations hesitate in this verse. The Hebrew is quite erotic, and most translators cannot bring themselves to bring out the obvious meaning. The smooth and expensively ornamented tusk of ivory is a loving description of her husband's erect penis."[27]

Did that just stop you in your tracks? Could God's Word really be that specific and erotic? There is nothing wrong with the powerful gift of sexual thought when it is channeled toward your own husband.

Your husband doesn't have to be on the cover of *GQ* for you to think sexually about him. What physical features do you love about him? His eyes, his hair, his shoulders? You fill in the blank. Or think of a time that you two shared great sexual passion. Remember what it felt like to be next to his naked body. You get the idea. This is why God created thoughts to be sexually powerful—not for erotic writers—for married lovers.

TAKE CREATIVE LICENSE

In Song of Solomon, the Smokin' Hot Mama used her creativity to plan a sexual field trip for her man.

Come, my love, let us go out to the fields
and spend the night among the wildflowers.
Let us get up early and go to the vineyards
to see if the grapevines have budded,
if the blossoms have opened,
and if the pomegranates have bloomed.
There I will give you my love.
There the mandrakes give off their fragrance,

and the finest fruits are at our door,
new delights as well as old,
which I have saved for you, my lover.
(Song of Solomon 7:11–13 NLT)

When the coded language of the Song is understood, you'll notice that this couple had a sexual encounter outside, in a vineyard. This is in the Bible! She told her husband, "I am storing up for you pleasures, both old and new." When is the last time you and your husband did something new, creative, and adventurous sexually?

You don't need erotica to give you permission or ideas of how to be creative. Use your imagination and learn how to have fun together.

During the busy years of babies and toddlers, I forgot what it was like to be creative, to be romantic, to be in love. If Mike hinted toward sex, I wanted to hide in a pile of laundry. I was too tired to even think about intimacy. At its very worst, I joked with my husband that we could have sex as long he didn't wake me up. We needed help and I knew it.

Both Mike and I are very competitive, so we used this to fuel creativity. We committed to two dates a month. I planned one, he planned the other. Because we were on a budget, each date had to be under twenty-five dollars. The challenge spurred us on not just to creativity but having fun again—in and out of bed. My two favorite memories were Mike's "Mission Impossible" date and my "fashion show" date. As for the details . . . well, those are classified.

SOUNDS LIKE FUN, BUT . . .

As you begin paving the way for great sex as a single woman, you have to address things differently because you don't have a sexual partner to play with. But I'm very happy that you—as a single woman—just read about the beauty of sexual pleasure. I believe one of the great failures of the church is programming women in singleness for sexual repression by hiding from them the notion that they are created to be sexual. That is not God's plan for purity.

PURITY IS NOT A NO—IT'S AN "OH YES!"

As a single woman, you also have a pathway to pleasure, but purity is the choice not to walk down it—yet. Purity is not a no. It is a "wait" for the sake of being able to say, "Oh yes!" In many other areas of our lives, we are able to accomplish this. To that late night hunger pang, we say, "Wait for breakfast" for the sake of saying yes to the smaller dress size. We say "wait" to our shop-'til-you-drop mentality to say yes to a vacation in Belize. But somehow, when it comes to sex, we can't think of it as "wait." We think it's a big no. Sexual desire was created by God and is very real. God doesn't want you to ignore it or white-knuckle your way through it.

The goal of purity is not sexual repression. We are, after all, sexual beings. Without any stimulation whatsoever, a woman will experience sexual desires in her everyday life. Approximately 40 percent of women will awaken sexually aroused[28] and possibly even having a spontaneous orgasm. This is called "nocturnal orgasm." It's natural and may be a part of God's design to release sexual tension, much like a wet dream for men. Don't be condemned by your own sexual sensations. They are not a symptom of impurity.

As an adult, single woman, you can be paving the way for deep intimacy and great sex in the future. Your choices now will have a significant impact, good or bad, on your sex life if and when the Lord brings a husband.

REMOVING THE BARRIERS

Many women wait until they are married to address sexual wounds or mistakes from their past. I've shared with you that I waited. I wanted to believe that my choices wouldn't impact my intimacy with Bob. For many years of marriage, I was navigating around huge boulders and stop signs in my pathway to pleasure. The biggest was in regard to memories of my past sexual partner. I want to share my secret to overcoming them, as promised, in the hope that it can help you with your memories.

After counseling hundreds of women, there is no doubt in my mind that there's a chemical and spiritual bond created with the people you have sex with. No way around it. Some people call these "soul ties." Others use words such as "enmeshment." But the very real bonding that occurs when you have sex with someone is not just emotional and spiritual but physiological.

One of the brain chemicals released during sex is dopamine. Dopamine makes you feel good; it creates a sense of peace and pleasure simultaneously. Anytime our bodies experience pleasure, the limbic system gets washed in dopamine. It doesn't matter if this is "good" pleasure—working out or having sex with your husband—or "bad" pleasure—doing crystal meth or having a great orgasm while you read erotica—dopamine sends signals to your brain to go back to the source of pleasure for more. In essence, it is the "craving" chemical. It makes you want more. It creates addiction. This addiction can be to having sex with your spouse. It can also be an addiction to porn or hooking up. (Neurochemicals are value neutral and don't care whether marital sex or erotica makes you feel good, they deluge the brain's receptors anytime the body feels pleasure.) But one thing is certain: dopamine "attaches" you to the source of pleasure.

Perhaps that's why the apostle Paul warned us: "Do you not know that he who unites himself with a prostitute is one with her in body? For it is said, 'The two will become one flesh'" (1 Corinthians 6:16). Lauren Winner says he's really writing: "Don't you know that when you sleep with someone, your body makes a promise whether you do or not?"[29] When I had sex with someone before I was married, my body made a promise. Years later, when I was in a happy marriage and enjoying my life, I could never really understand why I would think of this person when Bob and I fought (and only when we fought—never any other time).

One day my dear friend Lynn Nold asked me if I'd ever prayed to ask God to sever the bond that was created with my youthful sex partner. The truth is: I didn't know I needed to do that. But together Lynn and I knelt before God and asked Him to do just that. I can tell you that, although I didn't realize it for years, I never thought of that person again when Bob and I fought! And I have seen countless women experience similar healing.

If I were to tell you the two greatest steps in clearing my pathway to pleasure, they would be: (1) finally getting up the nerve to tell someone about my secret sin and (2) praying for God to break the bonding that occurred between me and my past partner. Have you experienced these two things? If not, they are a great place to begin. (You can find out more about this in my book *What Are You Waiting For? The One Thing No One Ever Tells You about Sex*, which includes information on how to pray for God to break the enmeshment of soul ties.)

The bottom line is this: sex is sacred and deserves incredible honor. We cannot afford to speak of it in hushed tones but must walk in full freedom regarding this beautiful gift from God. If we can do that well—as difficult as it may be—we will not only prepare the way for sexual fulfillment, but the world will see the love of God in the mystery of marriage. And that, as we'll show you in the next chapter, will also move us toward the goal of being spiritually satisfied!

"Marriage should be honored by all, and the marriage bed kept pure."

—Hebrews 13:4a

Pull Back the Shades

For both married and single women: If you have never taken time to confess your sexual sin to someone or to pray for God to break any bonding with past sexual partners, take steps to do that today. For married women: talk to your husband about how to implement some creativity in your marriage bed!

Chapter 8

The Spiritually Satisfied Woman

Perhaps it was painful for you to read the last chapter. Maybe you have questions like these women:

Will I always be alone? What am I saving myself for? I fear I'll never experience the love other women enjoy. What can I do to meet this deep sexual need?

Every night I sleep next to a man who hardly notices me. No one would guess how miserable we are. Will it ever change?

My life is so dull. Today is just like yesterday. Working, taking care of the kids, housework. There's no romance, no tingles, no satisfaction. Is the best part of my life over?

I don't think I will ever enjoy sex. What happened to me when I was a little girl has ruined it. Will I ever be healed?

Everything within us wants to promise these women a happy ending. We want to tell the single woman that God is preparing her for a wonderful man that she will someday wed. We want to guarantee the lonely, married woman that God will change the heart of her husband. We want to reassure the woman whose sex life has been ruined by childhood sexual abuse that all of her wounds will be instantly healed. But we can't make these promises because God doesn't make them—but sometimes the church does.

One very pure-hearted blogger was tired of empty promises for love and decided to slip off her "True Love Waits" ring as an adult when no husband was in sight. She wrote this:

> I had a poem on my bulletin board all through high school—the one where "God" was telling me to fall in love with Him first and then I would be able to fall in love with a husband later.
>
> Who wrote that poem anyway?
>
> Pretty sure it wasn't God.
>
> When Jesus was here on the earth, the crowds would follow Him because they saw He gave good things. But that's not what He wanted. He wanted their hearts for Himself. So He would turn to them and say things like, "If you don't love Me so much that every other relationship in your life looks like hate in comparison, you can't follow Me" (Matthew 10:34–39, paraphrased).
>
> That sounds a lot different from the poem.[30]

Let me be the first to say that the purity movement often romanticizes the hard work of faithfulness and self-respect by promising—maybe even guaranteeing—a man as a reward. God doesn't do that. And neither should we.

❖ ❖ ❖

It's about time someone told you the truth—a truth that you intuitively know but perhaps have been hesitant to accept: *Life is hard; not every longing you have on earth will be fulfilled.*

I bet you've never heard a sermon on what God does not promise. This is unfortunate because it is quite dangerous to place your trust in things you falsely assume God has promised. Jesus said that He came that you might have life and have it abundantly. His promises are great and He is trustworthy in fulfilling each one. But His ways are not our ways, and He has not promised some of the things you may have assumed or hoped He has.

Have you ever put money into a vending machine and been denied your snack or soda? In that moment of frustration, did you shake the machine to get your dangling chips to drop, or stick your hand up the opening to try to pry out the candy bar?

Often, we can treat God this way. We believe that if we have obeyed, He owes us our heart's desire. It's easy to fall into this trap because He *has* set forth principles of wisdom and morality that are supposed to make life go better. And a lot of times they do. The woman who works diligently on her marriage often falls more deeply in love with her man. The young woman who devotes herself to God and holiness often is rewarded with a godly husband. But not always.

What if God says no? What if He doesn't bring the husband, or the miracle, or the money, or the healing? What does that say about His love for you? Can you really trust Him to meet your deepest needs when you feel so unsatisfied?

DON'T CONFUSE GOD WITH WALT DISNEY

Not every good little girl will have a dashing man waiting to rescue her and ride off into the sunset, and not every marriage will be deeply intimate. Are there beautiful, God-ordained marriages? Absolutely! But remember those represent the gracious hand of God along with lots of hard work. Marriage is to be honored by all as a gift—not an entitlement.

I know this may sound like lame comfort if you are waiting, longing, and praying for God to bring the man of your dreams. But accepting that this desire may not be met will free you from the bondage of holding God to promises that He has never made.

Yes, God created you with deep longings to be loved by a man. He designed marriage to be intimate in every way. God made sex to be a powerfully pleasurable expression of married love. These are wonderful things to pray for and even hope *for*—but not things to place your hope *upon*. Your longings to be rescued by the white knight and to experience deep intimacy in marriage transcend having a wonderful husband. Those desires are meant to reflect your heart's deep yearning to be saved by the ultimate Bridegroom.

Have you ever realized that God's Word promises that Jesus will come on a white horse and will rescue His bride, that He is preparing a mansion for you and will one day wipe away every tear? These truths were written in Scripture thousands of years before fairy tales. The Cinderella story is just a shadow of a much greater spiritual longing. When marriage is healthy and men are truly honorable and chivalrous, this is a celebration of the ultimate Prince.

Yes, you are destined to be saved by the Prince. But His name is not Charming or Christian Grey. His name is Jesus. The blogger who slipped off her purity ring rightly came to the conclusion that "a lot of [single] girls were sold on a deal, not a Savior."

A THIRSTY WOMAN

The Bible records the story of Jesus' interaction with one unsatisfied, disillusioned, thirsty woman that we first mentioned back in chapter 1.

It's not much of a stretch to propose that Jesus intentionally sought out this specific woman for a conversation. (Perhaps like He is intentionally seeking you as you are reading this book.) John 4 records that He felt He "had to" go to Galilee and that He selected an unusual way to get there. Jesus broke many cultural and religious customs during this encounter.

At a well in Samaria, He met the woman. She came to get

water at the hottest part of the day, probably to avoid gossip and shame-filled glances. Why? She was a woman with sexual longings. Sexual secrets. Sexual shame. She had already been through five husbands and was currently living with another man. Each marriage apparently still left her thirsting for more.

Jesus wanted to talk to her about that thirst, so He asked her for some water. He doesn't seem to care about traditions or etiquette. Just that nagging thirst—not the one in His mouth, the one in her eyes.

> Jesus: "Will you give Me a drink?"
> The woman (with shock in her voice): "How can You ask *me* for a drink?"
> Jesus: "If you knew the gift of God and who it was that asked you, you would have asked Him and He would give you living water."
> (She's confused, so He clarifies.)
> Jesus: "Everyone who drinks this water will be thirsty again. (I imagine He gestures toward the well when He says that.) But whoever drinks the water I give them will never thirst. Indeed, the water I give them will become in them a spring of water welling in eternal life."

He knows her thirst for intimacy. The unmet longings. But He claims that He can satisfy them so completely that she'll never drag herself back to another sexual or relational counterfeit again. The story ends with her running off in enthusiastic joy to tell everyone she meets how dramatically different she is now that she has met Jesus.

This isn't just some nice Bible story. It is the account of a lonely woman whose life was changed. No matter your disappointment, your loneliness, and your past choices, Jesus offers you the same Living Water. He promises that if we drink from the water He gives, we'll be so satisfied that we'll never again have to seek a substitute. Not yet another husband. Not a live-in boyfriend. Not erotica. Not fantasy. His promise is that the Living Water will satisfy every thirst.

It will be enough.

We have found this to be true.

REAL INTIMACY IN HIS PRESENCE

It sounds superspiritual to claim that your relationship with Jesus can satisfy you so much that a loving man becomes an optional blessing, not a dire necessity. After all, can Jesus look into your eyes? Hold you in His arms? Tell you that you are beautiful? Can He really comfort you and protect you through the harsh realities of life? With your "Sunday school hat" on, you might say yes. But in reality, how can someone who physically isn't here be intimate with you?

For most of my childhood and much of my adulthood, living for Jesus was my duty. I wanted to obey Him in everything and I was afraid of doing something wrong. But there was a block when it came to love. I couldn't imagine that Jesus, the very Son of God who sits on His throne in heaven, would ever say my name, "Juli." I couldn't fathom that He could possibly take the time to know me intimately when there are so many billions of souls. I loved God but had no concept of what it meant to be intimate with Him. So I contented myself with being a dutiful servant for my Lord. I studied His Word and served Him faithfully but I looked for love from my husband, my parents, my children, and others.

Being in a position of public ministry, I had asked God to bring a mentor into my life. God brought Linda Dillow. Linda invited me on an overnight prayer and fasting retreat and she began to share with me her walk with the Lord. She said things like, "Jesus is my best friend. He's my Beloved. I just can't wait to get alone with Him and worship." I was intrigued. Was it really possible to have such a real and intimate relationship with God?

Listening to Linda, I felt like I was behind a fence, longing to be in the presence of Jesus, and she could walk into His presence anytime she wanted. I can't tell you how deeply I longed for this! I had a solid marriage, three sons, an international ministry at Focus on the Family, but I knew my heart wanted more. I was hungry, thirsty, famished, desperate to know my Savior like this. That night, after Linda went to bed, my soul sought the Lord like it never had. Here is some of what I wrote in my journal:

January 14, 2011

I seek You not because I am in pain or in obvious need, but because my soul is desperate to know more of You. I want to be consumed by You, Jesus, and to know the reality of Your holiness, the fullness of Your Spirit, to be Your beloved, and to lean on You as my best friend. I am Your servant, but not a lover of Jesus. People see me too much, they don't see You. May I hear the words of love You speak over me and may I worship You with all that I am! May I leave this place forever changed!!

There are tears in my eyes as I testify to you that my Jesus answered that plea. He immediately became so much more to me than a distant God or a faithful Master. He intimately became my Redeemer and Friend. Those who know me well can tell you that my life changed. Although I always served and obeyed God, I became absolutely and completely in love with Him. I longed to spend every free moment seeking Him, learning about Him, and worshiping my Lord.

I once heard a statement from Dr. Larry Crabb that caught my attention. "God is all I need, but I don't know Him well enough for Him to be all I have." I am learning the secret of knowing my Lord well enough that He is truly my hope and joy. This gives me the freedom to cherish every other gift, like my husband, my job, and my kids—without making them my lifeline.

THIRSTY NO MORE

The catalyst for my "well experience" was my struggling marriage and the inability to heal from my sexual past. If you think this seems a hopeless beginning, think again! A life of

125

desperation is just the right desert into which Jesus delights to bring His Living Water.

During this time, I was just getting to know our marriage counselor, Tippy. She had something I did not. She spoke of taking walks with Jesus just so they could talk, worshiping out loud each day in her home, and spending many hours a day in prayer.

I didn't even know how to spend fifteen minutes in prayer. During this time, God also led me to a book that challenged me to give up one full hour of my day to pray. That seemed impossible. I was a busy woman with a toddler and a baby to care for while I was working full-time and volunteering far more than I should have been. But I was desperately thirsty. I would try anything.

The first hour was one of the longest of my life. I didn't know how to fill it. The clock ticked by so slowly. But Tippy mentored me. Before too many weeks went by, I found myself immersed in worship songs for twenty or thirty minutes each day and devouring Bible studies for the rest of my hour. So dramatic was the transformation in me, that both my mother and my husband told me that it was like I found Jesus for the first time.

During those first weeks I wrestled in prayer with one thing more than any other: Was I truly forgiven of my sexual past and if I was, why did it still hurt so much? Jesus is not afraid to talk about sin. It is why He came. No matter the frequent advice I'd heard to let my sexual sin stay in the past, He was telling me to drag it into the light. He wanted me to break the facade of perfection and tell my counselor, my husband, and my mom about sin that I'd committed years ago. Those confessions mark the most terrifying moments of my life. And the most powerfully freeing. I had finally found the Living Water.

ARE YOU THIRSTY?

The story of this woman at the well ends this way:

Then, leaving her water jar, the woman went back to the town and said to the people, "Come, see a man who told me everything I ever did. Could this be the Messiah?" They came out of the town and made their way toward him. (John 4:28–30)

Do you long for the same Living Water that Juli, the Samaritan woman, and I found? You can have it! There are two powerful observations we'd like to make about how her story ended that may be helpful to you. It's time to begin to get practical in terms of *your* thirst.

1. She got honest. Jesus prompted her, of course. While they were talking, He asked her to go get her husband, knowing full well it would be an impossible request to fulfill. This enabled Him to ever so gently expose her sin. He knew there would be healing in this for her. There still is for us today. James 5:16 says, "Confess your sins to each other . . . so that you may be healed." Only Jesus can forgive us, but He has given us the body of Christ to facilitate our healing. Our minds are quick to think quite the opposite and we end up hiding our sin, but we promise you there is healing in transparency. I believe this was one of the keys to my own spiritual revival. Bob and I were very young, yet we were community leaders. We were also serving as the youth leaders of our church in the absence of a youth pastor. To put it more clearly, I worried about image management. How would it look if they knew what I had done? I mention this because so many women who've written to us struggling with erotica say that they can't tell anyone because "I'm the pastor's wife" or "My husband is the president of the largest bank in town." Let go of that or you may never experience the spiritual revival you desperately need. God wants you to be whole and often the way to that is through the brokenness. A great example is seen in this Samaritan woman who went to the well when no one else did to conceal her sin, but after she tastes Living Water, she's running through the streets rejoicing and inviting others to taste too. And she doesn't mind telling people: "He told me everything I ever did." (She wasn't talking about washing the dinner dishes!) Who have you told about your deepest darkest secrets? Maybe it's time to do that today. Find a wise, godly woman who will listen as you confess your secret struggles and sin, and you will be on your way to finding the Living Water.

2. She got bold. This woman leaves her jar behind, and boldly goes to tell the whole town about her encounter with the Savior. We'd like to ask you to get bold, too. Start by "leaving your jar behind." For you this might mean deleting a bunch of erotica from your e-reader or driving a stash of soft covers to the dumpster right now. It may mean breaking off a sinful relationship or asking that older, godly woman to help you set up accountability software for your computer. God's Spirit might be leading you to stop spending time with a man with whom you are developing unhealthy emotional connections. Or He could be asking you to stop dating a guy who doesn't share your faith. Don't stop short: go tell someone about your brave decision and the encounter you're having with Jesus as you pray through the content of this book. The boldness of telling someone just may be what keeps you from returning to your sin and living a satisfied life.

Throughout our years in ministry, we have had the privilege of getting to know many women who carry deep disappointment and pain, but are now deeply satisfied. Does this mean they never feel lonely or cry themselves to sleep? No. But they know where to go when the thirst returns . . . to the Living Water.

Maybe trusting God to meet your unmet longings (without the promise of Prince Charming) is a huge stretch for you. You can't imagine that a distant God could be so close to comfort and satisfy you. We understand. But you picked up this book for a reason. If all you do is read it and you don't roll up your sleeves to do something, you will have wasted your time.

An intimate walk with Jesus isn't reserved for "super Christians." He promises, "You will seek me and find me when you seek me with all your heart" (Jeremiah 29:13). You only have as much of God as you really want. So I ask, are you hungry for Him? Are you so thirsty for His love that you would dive headfirst into a well to be satisfied?

Pull Back the Shades

Take time to thoroughly pray through your
need for Living Water. We've written a
prayer for you or you can write one of your
own in your journal. The important thing
is to take time to confess both your sexual
sins and your deepest longings.

Lord Jesus,

I am thirsty for Living Water. My life is like that of the
woman You met at the well. I am using counterfeits to satisfy
my thirst, and they are not working. Help me in this time of
prayer to be honest and to bring every thought under Your
authority. Please forgive me for _____ (list
each sexual sin). Help me to direct my longings toward
You instead of toward _____ (list each longing that
is becoming an out-of-control thirst that is leading you to
sin). I believe Your Word when it says that we are healed
by confession. Please give me courage to tell _____
(be specific with the name of a counselor or mentor) about
my sin and struggles. I don't want to go back to the well of

my sin anymore. Please fill me with Your Living Water so that I will be satisfied.

In Jesus' name,

Amen

Maybe you are thirsty because you have never truly surrendered your life to Jesus. Have you ever consciously decided to make Him the one true God of your life? If you haven't, here is a prayer you can pray. Expect your life to change as He changes your heart, satisfying every deep need.

Dear Jesus,

I know that I am sinful and that my sin will eternally separate me from You. I long to know You here on earth and to live with You in heaven. Please forgive me for acting against Your designed intention for my life. I understand that I deserve death, but You died on the cross so that I can know eternal life with You. Please come live within me. Bring Your Living Water and begin to fill me. I surrender my life to You.

In Jesus' name,

Amen

Chapter 9

Reviving More
than Your Sex Life

The problem is not erotica—the problem is that we want to read it.

Our world is always going to offer us salacious temptation. We should expect it. But something is terribly wrong when Christian women embrace it.

What on earth is happening?

We think a story from across the pond tells it best.

In July 2012, Fox News reported that a hotel in England had replaced the bestselling book of all time with the fastest-selling book of all time: the Holy Bible was discarded for *Fifty Shades of Grey*.

> "Because everybody is reading *Fifty Shades of Grey*, we thought it would be a hospitable thing to do, to have this available for our guests, especially if some of them were a little bit shy about buying it because of its reputation," hotel owner Jonathan Denby told NBC News. Denby told NBC he found religious books a "wholly inappropriate" choice for private bedrooms in England's modern, secular society.[31]

The fact is that erotica may very well be replacing the Bible in many women's lives. Barna Group researchers reported that 9 percent of practicing Christians have read *Fifty Shades of Grey*, the same percentage of all Americans who have read the book. And among all American adults who read *Fifty Shades of Grey*, one in five were Christians.[32]

We're supposed to be making different choices and living a different kind of life than the rest of the world. While you certainly can and should celebrate your sexuality, there is also discretion required of the Christian woman who seeks to have her sex life be what God designed it to be: a picture of His passionate love for His people! God's Word clearly calls us to live our lives as He designed them to be lived in all areas, including sex. This demands that we choose a different path than the world's way. He calls us to holiness.

> As obedient children, do not conform to the evil desires you had when you lived in ignorance. But just as he who called you is holy, so be holy in all you do . . . live your lives as strangers here in reverent fear. (1 Peter 1:14–15, 17)

What happened? We are no longer set apart and holy.

THE RUBBLE OF A WALL

When we first began writing this book, we faced the challenges of writing it in two months. We had never written together and we lived across the country from each other.

Frankly, neither of us knew how it would be accomplished. We met together in Colorado Springs (where Juli lives) to seek the Lord's direction. On the first morning, we sat at Juli's kitchen table to unite ourselves in prayer. The first few moments went like this:

> Dannah: "Lord, thanks for opening my heart so dramatically as I read the book of Nehemiah this morning . . ."

> Juli, interrupting my prayer: "What? Wait! God brought me to Nehemiah this morning, too!"

Nehemiah! Not a common book like John or one appropriately full of sex and romance like Song of Solomon. God led both of us to abandon our current reading plans to get to this Old Testament book of history. We knew that God was uniting our hearts through this historical account of dramatic revival.

The book of Nehemiah begins with rubble. The wall of Jerusalem had been broken down in an assault pressing the people of God into exile. Over fifty years later, the Jewish people were scattered. Slowly, they returned. (Oh, how like our own lives and testimonies to be distant from God and come back slowly, tentatively!) By the time they returned, the walls were mere rubble, the gates had been burned with fire, and the people were "in great trouble and disgrace" (Nehemiah 1:3). It's difficult for us to appreciate why a wall was so critical to the holy city. In Nehemiah's day, the wall was important for two reasons. First, a wall was a boundary that set apart the

Israelite territory. Second, it served as the people's primary protection. Without the wall intact, nothing would physically distinguish the Israelites as God's distinct people, and they were open to constant attack and plunder.

We as God's people no longer have the physical security of a wall around us. However, we are still called to be set apart—for our protection. We believe there is to be an invisible wall of holiness around us today, too. It should let everyone know that we don't belong to this world. But it seems that today, as in Nehemiah's day, the wall has come down. There is very little spiritual discernment that sets apart Christian women from the world. As a result, there is rubble of ruin in the lives of so many. We are standing in rubble and we are in trouble and greatly disgraced. Someone has to do something. Could that someone be you?

SOMEBODY DO SOMETHING

Nehemiah was a respected man with an esteemed position in the government of Persia. He'd been raised in Persia; it was all he'd known. His life would have been just fine without the interruption of a call from God to tell him that His precious people in a distant land were in trouble. But Nehemiah's brother and some others who'd already gone back to Jerusalem came to him with a report of how terribly vulnerable and unprotected God's people were. It was time to rebuild. Nehemiah didn't stand around and complain, he decided to do something. It's easy to analyze, scrutinize, and talk about the problems with the church. What we need are people who—

like Nehemiah—will do something. We've been *pulling back the shades* and have presented you with some bad news about Satan's assault on God's women. Will you do something about it? If so, we believe that Nehemiah's response can direct your response. The Lord used him to change the course of history. We believe that the same Lord can equip each of us to change the spiritual direction of our homes, our churches, and our communities. But it all must begin, like it did for Nehemiah, with the condition of your own heart.

Let's look specifically at five aspects of Nehemiah's response. We believe that each of them cries out to us with a question about how we will respond to the current state of rubble within and around us.

1. Will you let the bad news pierce your heart?

When Nehemiah heard the bad news about Jerusalem, he was comfortably positioned in a prestigious role, living about a thousand miles away in Susa. Although it would be natural for him to feel badly about what was happening to his countrymen, he certainly could have viewed it as a "distant problem." After all, it didn't affect him personally.

Instead of just including the plight of his people in a passing prayer, Nehemiah allowed the bad news to absolutely devastate him. "When I heard this, I sat down and wept. In fact, for days I mourned, fasted, and prayed to the God of heaven" (Nehemiah 1:4 NLT). His distress wasn't just a fleeting stage. Four months later, he was still so grieved by the problem that his boss, the king, noticed his sadness.

Why was he so upset? Nehemiah accepted the spiritual burden of suffering for God's people. He chose to grieve, fast, and care about the plight of a city that he had probably never seen and people he had never met.

Even if erotica and other immorality haven't touched your home, they are destroying your brothers and sisters, rotting the integrity of God's people from the inside out.

As we have written this book, we have grieved many times. We've gotten up in the middle of the night to plead with God on your behalf. We've fasted. We've cried. Our invitation is for you to do the same.

Are you willing to allow this news to grieve you? It's not enough just to feel badly. Will you weep and mourn, fast and pray in response to what you now know?

2. Will you begin with personal repentance?

Nehemiah's response to the bad news was not a patronizing prayer for his brothers nor was it an angry demand that God do something to fix the situation. Not only did he take the crisis personally, he took responsibility for it. Nehemiah recognized that Jerusalem's plight was the result of their sin and rebellion. Even though he didn't live there, he identified with the sinfulness of his people and he repented.

> I confess the sins we Israelites, including myself and my father's family, have committed against you. We have acted very wickedly toward you. (Nehemiah 1:6–7)

Do you realize how radical this is? Our human nature is to minimize and deny our own sin. Nehemiah, along with many of the great men of the Bible, went the next step and took personal responsibility for the sinfulness of his own family and countrymen. He understood that the "rubble" of sin must be removed before God could ever start rebuilding.

For the first decade of my marriage, I was very concerned about my husband's purity—what he might be thinking about or looking at. I spent a lot of time praying that God would protect him and keep his sexuality focused on me. When I had three boys, I became paranoid about raising them in this sexually explicit world. One day, I had my sons with me as I checked out at the grocery store. I noticed the *Sports Illustrated* swimsuit edition right at my oldest son's eye level. I was irate! Like a mama bear defending her cubs, I complained to the checkout lady. When she did nothing, I complained to the store manager. When he did nothing, I threatened to take my business elsewhere. The manager replied, "That's fine, lady, but you'll find this magazine in every store in the city." I was fighting a losing battle!

When God took me through my own personal revival, the nature of the battle changed completely. I stopped worrying about my husband and my kids, I stopped yelling at store managers, and I started getting on my knees—every day—in repentance. I repented for my sin, for my pride, for my independence, my stubbornness, and begged the Lord that I might walk in His mercy that day and every day. This has had a greater impact on my husband, my children, and my circle of influence than anything I've ever said or done.

Personal repentance paves the way for God to work both in and through us.

3. Will you take a risk to be God's instrument for change?

Nehemiah's despair and repentance went beyond his own personal prayer during his "quiet time." The burden for his people became so great that he took action. Nehemiah used his position of influence to ask the king for permission to go to Jerusalem to rebuild the walls. Then he asked for safe passage and building materials.

Please note that this was not like Nehemiah asking his boss for vacation time so he could go on a short-term mission trip. He risked his life by making such a request. His boldness came from the great burden, nurtured over four months of praying, fasting, repenting, and asking the Lord to act on his behalf. Nehemiah records, "Because the gracious hand of my God was upon me, the king granted my requests" (Nehemiah 2:8).

When you allow God to nurture your burden for His people, the time will surely come to step out in faith. A few years ago, the Lord began to burden my heart for women who are in sexual bondage. This included women who had been sexually abused, those who were frustrated by no intimacy in marriage, and those who were running to the world for answers that only God can provide. I began to plead and beg for God to do something for these women. "God, why

140

don't You do something?!" Then one day, I heard the Lord respond, "Juli, why don't *you* do something?"

At the time, I had my dream job as the cohost of the Focus on the Family radio broadcast. I was in ministry and impacting lives. But the burden for women became so great that I couldn't sit comfortably in a studio behind a microphone. My heart physically ached with the burden God had given me. Within a year, I resigned my position at Focus on the Family to begin a ministry for women called Authentic Intimacy.

Did I risk my life like Nehemiah? No. And you probably won't have to either. But at some point, it will cost you to stand boldly for revival. It may cost your reputation, a job, money, your health, or your comfort. Are you ready?

4. Are you willing to fight the opposition?

Even though the gracious hand of the Lord was leading Nehemiah, he still had many obstacles to face. His enemies taunted, manipulated, threatened, and deterred Nehemiah in every way imaginable. He even had his own team fighting against him at certain points as rich Jews began profiteering from the rebuilding and Nehemiah had to confront his own people! Through it all, Nehemiah consistently prayed and worked, trusting that God was greater than the opposition. At one point in the building process, the threats became so great that everyone building the wall worked with a weapon in one hand and the building tools in the other hand. In our world today, you might think of this as praying (holding a weapon) while you work (holding a tool).

Theologian Dr. J. Sidlow Baxter draws this principle from Nehemiah, "There is no winning without working and warring. There is no opportunity without opposition . . . Whenever the saints say, 'Let us arise and build,' the enemy says, 'Let us arise and oppose.' . . . There is a cross in the way of every crown that is worth wearing."[33]

Satan *hates* revival. He will use anything and anyone at his disposal to discourage it. If you pursue revival, in your own heart and beyond, expect opposition—both from secular sources and even from those who call themselves Christians.

LEARNING HOW TO FIGHT

When Juli first approached me to work with her on this book, I was already bloodied and bruised from a battle to bring sexual and spiritual revival to secular college campuses. If you haven't noticed, the message of purity isn't one that gets a lot of tolerance at most public universities. I expected opposition from those who do not know Jesus but was surprised at the number of Christians who were opposed to our work. How deep the wounds can be when they come from friendly fire! While I prayed about if I wanted to fight another battle—writing this book—I felt God inviting me to put on the armor of God and to pick up my weapon of warfare. In one year, I've moved from being a woman who teaches purity to tweens and teens— something even the most liberal thinkers often applaud me for doing—to fighting two battles that put me squarely against believers who accept the sexual climate of college campuses and embraced—applauded even—the Fifty Shades of Grey series. I'm not a confrontational person, and this has been uncomfortable for me, but there's a reason to stay in the battle.

◆ ◆ ◆

Just last week I was speaking at a live event where I challenged the teen girls and their mothers to "confess your sins to each other . . . so that you may be healed" (James 5:16). At the end of the event, the most innocent little redhead came up to me with a big smile. The baby-white skin on her cheeks was spotted with dainty freckles. She looked to be fourteen or fifteen. As she quickly approached me, her smiled melted into uncontrollable tears that contorted her once life-giving smile into a haunted expression.

"I confessed something to my mom," she blurted. "My sin is reading sexual stories online. I'm addicted and have been for two years."

Two years! Was she twelve when she began reading erotica?

My mind wrestled with the tragedy of it as I held her and she wept in my arms.

I grieved that night. Lamenting with my friends, my heart entered into an entirely new place in this battle as I realized how young some of the victims can be.

Listen, I know you may be bloodied and bruised from other battles. I know your schedules are filled to the brim with good things—even godly things. Neither Juli nor I really wanted to fight this battle. But we were called to it.

And so are you, my friend.

◆ ◆ ◆

5. Will you return to the truth of God's Word?

Nehemiah didn't just rebuild a physical wall to protect Jerusalem. He, along with Ezra the scribe, rebuilt the spiritual wall of clinging to God's truth and calling the people to be spiritually set apart. God's Law provided the protection and spiritual distinction just as the physically rebuilt walls had done. As the Israelites celebrated their new wall, Ezra stood before all the people and read God's Law. "He read it aloud from daybreak till noon . . . in the presence of the men, women and others who could understand. And all the people listened attentively to the Book of the Law" (Nehemiah 8:3). How attentively? Nehemiah 8:5 says that they stood up when the Word was read. They gave it their full attention. "Ezra praised the Lord, the great God; and all the people lifted their hands and responded, 'Amen! Amen!' Then they bowed down and worshiped the Lord with their faces to the ground" (Nehemiah 8:6). Theirs was a full body response to God's Word. Standing. Bowing. Worshiping!

When the apostle Paul tells us to put on the full armor of God to fight our battles, he mentions only one weapon of offense: the Word of God, which is called the "sword of the Spirit." Since we are reclaiming territory currently in the hands of the enemy, none of us can go into the battle without this vital tool! We haven't.

We began most of our writing and editing times by prayerfully reading the Word. Why? Because we don't want to give you our opinion—we want to share with you God's truth.

How about you? Has Fifty Shades or any other material replaced God's Word as the source of truth or comfort in your life? When God rebuilt Jerusalem, He revived His people's hunger and reverence for His Word. Today God wants to build a wall of truth around you, equipping you to live in this world with love and holiness!

Use the sword of the Spirit! Here are some offensive weapons in case you need them. Write them on index cards today and start reading them in the authoritative posture of standing.

Psalm 13:2

Psalm 19:13–14

Proverbs 2:12–19

Proverbs 5:1–23

Proverbs 6:24–29

Proverbs 7:1–27

1 Corinthians 10:13

2 Corinthians 10:5

James 1:14–15

2 Timothy 2:22

Hebrews 3:1

1 Timothy 4:12

1 Timothy 5:2

Colossians 3:2–7

Galatians 5:24–25

Philippians 4:7

ARE YOU READY TO GET IN THE GAME?

This book is not ultimately about the Fifty Shades series or even about erotica. This book is about the spiritual battle for the hearts and souls of women. Our prayer is not just that you throw out the junk that enslaves you to the world's thinking but that you join a call for revival among God's women.

What do you think of when you read the word *revival*? Do you get a picture in your head of tent meetings? Revival is, in fact, old-fashioned. We have not seen a true revival in over one hundred years. In our lifetime, we only know a world that is getting worse. We've grown so accustomed to eroding moral standards that we can't even conceive of a total reversal of that momentum. But it can happen.

The Welsh revival of 1904–1905 resulted in restaurants and stores closing from noon until two so that people could focus on prayer and fasting (Can you imagine the mall closing so we could pray?). Bars, nightclubs, and strip joints closed their doors for lack of clientele. (In one town the saloon sold only nine cents worth of liquor on a Saturday night.) And the Bible? You couldn't find one to buy! They were sold out!

The name most associated with the Welsh revival is Evan Roberts. Leading up to the revival, he spent seven hours a day in prayer and was overcome with the will of God for his life. Revival began with him because he was revived. In the course of one year, nearly 100,000 new believers followed Christ, and revivals were sparked in several other nations as a result of what started with one man. At the age of twenty-four, he'd been nothing more than a coal worker with no influence, age, or strategy. He wasn't even a licensed minister. He was just willing to be God's instrument.

Revival is not about holding our ground—it's about re-claiming territory that has already been lost. Can you imagine a day in which the divorce rate is dramatically lower? Or reading there is an astounding decrease in everything from cohabita-tion to sexually active teens? Or hearing about porn produc-ers, strip clubs, and writers of erotica going out of business because no one is interested in what they offer? Does it even seem possible?

We are praying and fighting for a revolution—*and* to be clear, it is both a spiritual and sexual revival. If marriage is a picture of God's love for the church, sex matters very much. It's time to stop just playing defense, assuming that the best we can do is hold our ground. We serve and worship a God who is able to not just hold back the tide of evil but to usher in a reign of righteousness and holiness. Now is the time to beg God to equip us to kick the enemy out and to take back what he has stolen.

Wake up!

We've got a wall to build.

Pull Back the Shades

We've shared with you how the Lord has called us to respond personally to work on "building a wall." What about you? What specific step can you take to respond to what the Lord has shown you about your own heart? About the plight of Christian women?

QUESTIONS FOR GROUP DISCUSSION

Chapter 1

1. What is your opinion about the five longings Juli and Dannah discussed? Do you think they accurately express why women are drawn to erotica?
2. Where in the Bible do you see each of these longings validated?
3. Talk about how each legitimate need has been tarnished by the world's system of thought.
4. Which unmet longing do you personally identify with the most?

Chapter 2

1. Discuss how moral and spiritual laws are changed in erotic literature. Why is this dangerous?
2. Share about a time when you thought you could "beat the consequences" of immoral or foolish behavior.
3. How can you discern if a book or movie is inspiring you toward discontentment?
4. Read Philippians 4:12–13. Why is contentment so important to spiritual growth and joy?

Chapter 3

1. What do you think about the thesis that "mommy porn is spiritual"? Do you agree? Why or why not?

2. Why do you think Satan has such a great agenda to destroy and distort sexuality?

3. Discuss ways that our world has made an idol out of "romantic love." Describe a way that you've fallen for this.

4. If mommy porn is spiritual, what practical steps can you take to make sure you are on the right side of the battle?

Chapter 4

1. What are some areas where you see confusion about what is right and wrong in the area of sexuality?

2. What do you think about the four questions (Paul's filter) that help you decide if something is right or wrong? Would you add another?

3. Talk about the Enemy's agenda to paint God as the "killjoy." Read Genesis 3:1–6. How does this strategy still apply today?

4. If a Christian friend asked you if you thought reading Fifty Shades was okay, how would you answer?

Chapter 5

1. Why do you think sexual practices like BDSM are becoming commonplace in our culture?

2. Talk about the tension of wanting a strong man but not wanting to be controlled.

3. Read Genesis 3:16. How do you think this passage applies to the discussion?

4. What do you think of Dannah and Juli's thoughts on "healthy power"? Do you agree or disagree?

Chapter 6

1. A married friend of yours says, "I read erotica because it makes me want sex with my husband." Based on what you read in this chapter, how would you respond?

2. Do you believe there is a difference between erotica and porn? Why or why not? Why do you think erotica is more "acceptable" in Christian circles than pornography?

3. How would you explain to someone (married or single) that a sexual release alone is a poor substitute for intimacy?

4. What practical steps can you take toward true intimacy in your life—with God, with your husband, with your community?

Chapter 7

1. Why do you think many Christian women have difficulty feeling sexually unrestrained in marriage?

2. Why does the struggle to experience sexual freedom make books like Fifty Shades more attractive to Christian married women?

3. What would it look like for the Christians to play "offense" instead of just "defense" in the battle for sexuality? As a married woman, what does it look like to play "offense"?

4. As a single woman, how might you hold to a standard of purity while also acknowledging that your sexuality is a good thing? What does this look like practically?

Chapter 8

1. Do you think it's unrealistic to believe that your relationship with Jesus can meet your needs for intimacy? Why or why not?
2. G. K. Chesterton once wrote, "Every man who knocks on the door of a brothel is looking for God." Talk about how his observation applies to the popularity of Fifty Shades.
3. Read the account of the woman at the well in John 4:1–26. What is the most profound aspect of this account for you personally?
4. You read Dannah's and Juli's testimonies of how they took a step toward being filled with the Living Water of Jesus. What step might the Savior be asking you to take?

Chapter 9

1. Throughout this book, you've read about some very bad news related to the assault against Christian women. How has this "news" touched you personally?
2. Read Nehemiah chapter 1. How did the "bad news" affect Nehemiah? How does his response challenge you personally?

3. The workers who rebuilt the wall in Jerusalem were often assigned to begin by rebuilding the section of wall in front of their own home or neighborhood. They began at home. How do you need to begin rebuilding a "wall of holiness" in your own home?
4. What is the Lord specifically asking you to do in response to the "broken walls of holiness" around His women?

Appendix 1

Practical Resources

dirtygirlsministries.com
Crystal Renaud
An online accountability community for women overcoming sexual addiction, especially porn or erotica.

X3pure.com
An online thirty-day recovery program featuring confidential, streaming video workshops.

covenanteyes.com
Accountability software for your computers and some mobile devices.

safeeyes.com
Blocking software for your computers and some mobile devices.

passionatecommitment.com
Dr. Cliff and Joyce Penner
Sex therapy from a Christian perspective.

BOOKS AND STUDIES

Braddock Bromley, Nicole. *Hush: Moving from Silence to Healing After Childhood Sexual Abuse.* Chicago: Moody, 2007.

For survivors of abuse, this book will help you to understand what you've experienced and how you can move on for further healing.

Dillow, Linda, and Dr. Juli Slattery. *Passion Pursuit: What Kind of Love Are You Making?* Chicago: Moody, 2013.

Passion Pursuit is a 10-week, DVD-driven Bible study for married women taught by Linda Dillow and Dr. Juli Slattery. It includes a workbook with five days of homework for each week, designed to take you into God's holy Word and apply the principles to your marriage.

Gresh, Dannah. *And The Bride Wore White: Seven Secrets to Sexual Purity.* Chicago: Moody, 2004, 2012.

And the Bride Wore White is a book written for teens that has an accompanying ten-week leader's guide so that it can be used as a Bible study. It instills a solid biblical foundation for purity into young women.

Moore, Beth. *Breaking Free.* **Nashville: B&H, 2007.**

> This is a fantastic Bible study that can be used as a tool to help you reprogram your mind. Does not deal specifically with sexuality, but many have used it in their journey to freedom.

Appendix 2

What Do I Do with My Struggle? Practical Ideas for Victory

Whether you are married or single, your sexual appetite will be influenced by what you choose to think about. We've made the point that reading erotica, watching sexually explicit movies, or fantasizing about some "superman" will spoil your healthy longings for intimacy. But how do you stop? Here are a few practical tips to help you in your journey.

Identify the triggers that make you vulnerable. When are you most sexually tempted? When you feel lonely? bored? hurt? anxious? Do you notice any predictable patterns? If so, find healthy ways to meet these longings. We know one single mom who noticed that when the darkness of night fell—her trigger—she was prone to romantic fantasy and so made the decision to set her alarm and get up early each day so she'd be too tired to do anything but sleep when night came. If you are single and the longing for physical touch is a trigger, schedule a regular massage. If stress seems to be your trigger, go for a run, which can be effective at offering your brain some of the same chemicals to reduce stress that sex would.

Limit your access to sources of temptation. Do the practical things like putting a filter on your computer and getting rid of books or movies that get your mind going in the wrong direction. Break off any relationship that is built on lust or causes you to want what God hasn't given you.

Set up accountability. One of the most difficult things to do may be to admit to someone else that you are struggling. When you take this step and ask a godly friend or mentor to keep you accountable, you have taken a giant step in winning the battle.

Change Your Appetite. Crystal Renaud, a single woman and founder of dirtygirlsministries.com, coaches women who want to overcome an addiction to porn or erotica. One of her clients, Charlotte, could not be aroused with her husband unless she first used erotica. They needed to restore a healthy appetite to this woman. This required her to fast for a time from sex *entirely* and to focus on her friendship with her husband (read: *intimacy*). While we would not recommend such a fast to many married women, Charlotte's dependence on erotica had dismantled her ability to be ultimately aroused and fulfilled by her husband. During this season, Charlotte was in regular counseling and had a phone number to call when she felt tempted to use erotica. On a more positive note, she was assigned to spend focused time enjoying conversation and friendship with her husband who was supporting her in this period of abstinence.

At the end of the fast, they set a special date and reserved a hotel room. That night, for the first time in her life, she was orgasmic with her husband—free from any fantasy—and now she is able to do that on a regular basis. Erotica promised her more but left her unsatisfied. A healthier pathway to her desires delivered just what she needed to be satisfied.

This ability to have your sexual appetite balanced through fasting is also key for singles. Fasting as a single woman means refusing to ignite your sexual appetites with counterfeits that only leave you craving more. Not what you wanted to hear? We promised you we'd tell you the hard truth. Don't think it's any easier to manage the challenges as a married woman. Here's how Paul speaks that hard truth for all of us:

> I do . . . tell the unmarried and widows that single-ness might well be the best thing for them, as it has been for me. But if they can't manage their desires and emotions, they should by all means go ahead and get married. The difficulties of marriage are preferable by far to a sexually tortured life as a single. (1 Corinthians 7:8–9 THE MESSAGE)

His one outlet for sexual tension remains marriage. Period. (And isn't it fitting that he is quick to remind those seeking that outlet that it's full of difficulties as well?)

Build intimacy in core relationships. Genesis 2:18 says, "It is not good for the man to be alone." Based on this verse, the Christian world often jumps to the conclusion that sin-gleness is *not* good. But the verse doesn't say it's not good for man to be sexually abstinent or unmarried. It says it's not good for him to be *alone*. Your desire for sex is not just a drive for a physical release but a force meant to propel you to seek intimacy. The authors of *Authentic Human Sexuality* describe sexual desire in the context of a drive to community:

> Deeply embedded within each one of us is a divine longing for wholeness that sends us reaching beyond ourselves and to God and others. Sexual desire helps us recognize our incompleteness as human beings and causes us to seek the other to find a fuller meaning in life . . . Authentic sexuality urges us towards a rich sharing of our lives.[34]

How are you *sharing your life*? Here are some suggestions:

As a Single

Through healthy relationships with coworkers, lunch dates with friends, small groups, and a life fueled with purpose in charitable works, you may find that you enjoy a great deal of emotional intimacy that's so necessary to fulfilled living. And living in intimacy now is great practice for living in intimacy with your life partner. Here are some ideas for you:

Get out your fine china and start hosting dinner parties!

Schedule weekly accountability meetings with an older, wiser woman.

Learn something new with a good friend. Tennis. Horseback riding. Oil painting. The process of exposing yourself to risk and learning is intimate!

Dare to tell a very trustworthy friend some of your deepest, most treasured secrets this week. Invite her in to your inner thought life.

In Marriage

Have a date night. It can be nearly impossible to fit your friendship into the to-do list and fast pace of family life and home ownership.

Make a "bucket list" together. Every year, work together to knock one or two items off the list.

Find a local nonprofit you can work at together. It can be anything—a short-term missions trip, working in the church nursery, or serving Thanksgiving dinner to the needy.

Take up a new hobby together. Be creative. Take an Asian cooking class, join a gym together, or learn to paint landscapes. Research shows that couples who do new things together have greater long-term satisfaction in their marriage.

Authentic intimacy requires community but does not always require sex. God created you to function in community whether single or married. This is what makes your human sexuality so drastically different from the physical urges and fertile expression of the rest of the animal world.

No woman has ever died from not having sex or from the lack of great sex in marriage. But you cannot live as God intended without deep connection.

NOTES

1. Barbara Walters quoted in Joyce Chen, "Barbara Walters stuns 'View' panel, asks co-host Elisabeth Hasselbeck: 'Do you like it when he's rough?'" *New York Daily News*, April 16, 2012. www.nydailynews.com/entertainment/tv-movies/barbara-walters-stuns-view-panel-asks-co-host-elisabeth-hasselbeck-rough-article-1.1062939.

2. John and Stasi Eldredge, *Captivating* (Nashville: Thomas Nelson, 2005), 9.

3. EL James, "Fifty Shades of Success: Behind the (Sex) Scenes with E. L. James," interview by Marlo Thomas, *Huffington Post*, October 4, 2012. www.huffingtonpost.com/marlo-thomas/fifty-shades-of-success_b_1923039.html.

4. EL James, *Fifty Shades of Grey* (New York: Vintage Books, 2011), 245.

5. Ibid., 485.

6. Ibid., 488.

7. Ibid., 491.

8. Ibid., 490 (those italics are from the book—not me).

9. Timothy Keller, *Counterfeit Gods* (New York: Riverhead, 2011), xviii.

10. Ibid., 29.

11. EL James, *Fifty Shades Darker* (New York: Vintage Books, 2012), 414.

12. Ibid., 454.

13. EL James, *Grey*, 292–94.

14. EL James, "Fifty Shades of Success."

15. Linda Dillow and Dr. Juli Slattery, *Passion Pursuit* (Chicago: Moody, 2013), 101–2.

16. EL James, *Grey*, 422.

17. http://abcnews.go.com/Health/bdsm-advocates-worry-fifty-shades-grey-sex/story?id=17369406.

18. Though not quoted directly, the definitions used in this paragraph were taken from Wikipedia pages including: http://en.wikipedia. org/wiki/BDSM, http://en.wikipedia.org/wiki/Sexual_submission, and http://en.wikipedia.org/wiki/Top_(BDSM).

19. EL James, *Grey*, 169–70.

20. One San Francisco sex store saw a 65 percent increase in bondage gear just a few months after the release of *Fifty Shades of Grey* in the U.S. http://articles.chicagotribune.com/2012-07-24/features/ sc-fam-0724-sex-toys-20120724_1_toy-sales-bondage-and-disci-pline-shades.

21. EL James, *Darker*, 412–13.

22. Michael Young, Denny George, Tamera Young, Raffy Luquis, "Sexual Satisfaction among Married Women," *American Journal of Health Studies*, March 22, 2000. Retrieved March, 2013, at http:// www.highbeam.com/doc/1G1-72731720.html.

23. Dr. Allan Meyer, *From Good Man to Valiant Man* (Mt. Evelyn, Australia: self-published, 2008), 61.

24. Kyrsty Hazell, "Fifty Shades of Grey: Erotic Novel Sparks Increase in Extramarital Bondage," *Huffington Post*, July 10, 2012. www.huffingtonpost.co.uk/2012/07/10/sex-fifty-shades-of-grey-effect-bondage-trend_n_1662122.html.

25. Michael Young, Denny George, Tamera Young, Raffy Luquis, "Sexual Satisfaction."

26. Robert T Michael et al., *Sex in America: A Definitive Survey* (Boston: Warner Books, 2007), 157.

27. Dan B. Allender and Tremper Longman III, *Intimate Allies* (Carol Stream, IL: Tyndale, 1999), 254.

28. Barbara L. Wells, "Predictors of Female Nocturnal Orgasms: A Multivariate Analysis," *The Journal of Sex Research* 22, no. 4 (November 1986). Retrieved March 28, 2013, from highbeam.com.

29. Lauren F. Winner, *Real Sex* (Grand Rapids: Brazos Press, 2006), 88.

30. Anonymous, "I Don't Wait Anymore," *Grace for the Road*, February 3, 2012. http://gracefortheroad.com/2012/02/03/idontwait/.

31. Fox News, "Hotel replaces bible with '50 Shades of Grey,'" July 25, 2012. www.foxnews.com/travel/2012/07/25/hotel-replaces-bible-with-50-shades-grey-420750936/#ixzz2LlUGpiEl.

32. Barna Group, "The Books Americans Are Reading," Barna Group, June 4, 2013. www.barna.org/barna-update/culture/614-the-books-americans-are-reading#.UswRIvRDt6c.

33. Dr. J. Sidlow Baxter, *Explore the Book, Volume 2* (Grand Rapids: Zondervan, 1986), 230–31.

34. Judith K. Balswick and Jack O. Balswick, *Authentic Human Sexuality* (Downers Grove, IL: InterVarsity Press, 1999), 41.

Acknowledgments

The invisible woman behind this project is Terry Behimer, our editor. Thank you, Terry, for your prayer, direction, and encouragement!

Thanks to Holly Kisly, René Hanebutt, and the rest of the Moody publishing team for giving us the green light on this project and working to get it into women's hands.

There are many women who have prayed for us as we were writing. Thank you for the protection and the strength the Lord provided through your prayers!

Finally, we want to thank our husbands, Bob and Mike. Writing a book like this puts our marriages on the "front lines" of the battle. We absolutely couldn't and wouldn't have tackled this project without you.

PASSION PURSUIT

978-0-8024-0639-2

Can sex be holy and erotic? Does God have an opinion about sex? What's okay in the bedroom? This audaciously bold ten-week bible study and DVD curriculum will answer these and many other questions that women have but haven't had a trusted source for honest, biblical answers. Now they do.

Also available as an ebook

MOODY
PUBLISHERS

www.MoodyPublishers.com

AND THE BRIDE
WORE WHITE

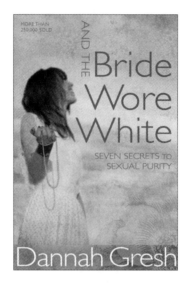

978-0-8024-0813-6

In *And The Bride Wore White*, Dannah share passages from her journals that show the joy and heartache of her own dating years — the challenges and temptations, successes and failures. She exposes Satan's lies about sex, shares a three-step plan to breaking off harmful relationships, provides compassionate guidelines for healing, and offers seven secrets of sexual purity to apply to your life.

Also available as an ebook

MOODY
PUBLISHERS

www.MoodyPublishers.com

authentic intimacy

bringing God's truth to women

A MINISTRY OF LINDA DILLOW & DR. JULI SLATTERY

We declare God's Truth in areas of a woman's life that the enemy has twisted. Through writing, speaking, podcasts, blogs, and our website, we are reclaiming God's design for intimacy in a way that translates into a woman's daily life. We are a ministry that discusses questions Christian women have, but aren't sure where to go for answers. Authentic Intimacy is audaciously bold, courageously real, and decidedly Biblical.

www.AuthenticIntimacy.com

Connect to Authentic Intimacy through our website, Pinterest, Facebook, and Twitter

Brewing rich conversations, delivering bold truth.

Pour yourself a cup of coffee and enjoy **Java with Juli**, a new podcast by host and clinical psychologist Dr. Juli Slattery. From the cozy setting of a coffee shop, Juli offers a woman's perspective on intimacy and converses with guests about the challenges of being a contemporary Christian woman.

www.moodyradio.org/javawithjuli